Dedication

*To my parents Lalitha and Ramaswamy,
my husband Amit and my daughter Samara.*

*To the people who made this journey possible in
every little way – Coach Vivek Menon, Coach Penni,
Coach Jay, Coach Rajeev Char, Coach Rama, Ashok
Someshwar and the entire Mumbai Road Runners'
Community.*

*This book is also dedicated to all my Professors
at Stanford under whose able guidance I took
the creative writing courses and of course to my
classmates at Stanford.*

A TURBULENT MIND

A TURBULENT MIND

My Journey to Ironman 70.3

Swetha Amit

First published in 2020

Publishing Facilitation: AuthorsUpFront

 **The Write Place**
A Publishing Initiative by Crossword Bookstores Ltd.
Umang Tower, 2nd Floor, Mindspace, Off Link Road,
Malad West, Mumbai 400064, India.

Web: www.TheWritePlace.in
Facebook: TheWritePlace.in
Twitter: @WritePlacePub
Instagram: @WritePlacePub

Author's Note

Sometimes in life, you are hit by an unexpected wave of change. A change that will forcibly stir you out of your cocooned comfort zone. You may face despair, loneliness and depression. This is not a dead end but just a test to rediscover yourself and unleash your inner potential. These struggles may help you metamorphose into a new identity.

During that one year at Stanford, I faced all of the above and did not allow myself to wallow into a pool of depression. Instead, I chose a different path to channelize my mind and discover myself in the process. Different people have different ways of coping with low phases in their lives, for me it was a triathlon and eventually the Ironman 70.3 race.

I don't come from an athletic background and yet I surprised myself by doing something that I thought was beyond my reach. I hope this book resonates with all those aspiring triathletes to pursue their dreams. It is not easy as it comes with its share of challenges. However, it is never too late to start, nor is it never too late to learn swimming, ride a bike or start running. Age is just a number. You never know what you are capable of unless you give it a try. So never stop trying or rather 'tri'ing.

Disclaimer: The triathlon training plan mentioned in some of the chapters is not a universal plan to be followed by everyone. It is a customized plan given to me by Coach Viv based on my fitness levels and certain time trials for each discipline. I would advise people to not follow it blindly. Always approach a certified triathlon coach who would help you devise a proper training plan for a triathlon, based on your fitness levels and goals.

Foreword

I have been training, racing and coaching endurance events for many years. Triathlons have been the most challenging ones. Very few can Swim, Bike and Run, let alone claim to be good at all three. As recreational triathletes, it is not just about balancing your training to get the optimum results, it also involves juggling your work and family life. More often than not your social life takes a back seat and weekends are spent grinding out a long bike and run workout.

Training for long-distance triathlons, such as the Half Iron and Full Iron distance, is a journey in itself. It teaches you to be consistent, focused on your goal, overcome mind games as well as to fight any inner demons. Most of us take up this challenge to prove the impossible, to travel into the unknown and to emerge triumphant, and in doing so a few of us fall in love with this amazing sport.

The triathletes that I coach take up this sport for

different reasons. But there is one common trait in all, the willingness to do what is needed to reach the finish line.

Swetha has been a friend first and then a mentee. When she spoke with me about attempting a triathlon, there was a fear of the unknown, but at the same time a resolve to finish one. The approach was to test the waters with smaller distances before taking the plunge into a Half Iron. During that journey, she overcame her biggest fear, that was of swimming in the open waters. There were days when she questioned her ability to bike, or the worry that her run was getting slower or many things that she tried for the first time.

During her entire journey, there wasn't a single day when I doubted her ability to finish the race. I knew it wouldn't be easy, but I also knew that she would cross the finish line. For those of you who are thinking about getting into this sport, this book will motivate you to take that plunge. And for the rest of us triathletes, you will find a part of yourself in the chapters of this book. Happy reading and keep 'Tri'-ing!

Vivek Menon
Ironman Certified Coach
Mumbai, India

Contents

Chapter 1

The Wave of Trepidation

"The fears we don't face become our limits."
– Robin Sharma

The race day had dawned. I got up with that one thought which was constantly nagging my mind. Would I complete the Ironman 70.3 race?

Not exactly the ideal thought to have on a race morning. My heart felt as though a thousand moths were flapping their wings. This same feeling I had experienced during my final exams in school. My future had depended on my performance. Yet this Ironman race wasn't the determinant of my future. Barring the professionals, it was just another race for many. So why did it feel as though this race was a do or die situation for me? All I knew was that if I didn't finish this race, those inner demons would continue to haunt me. The ghosts of failure would taunt me for the rest of my life. I would probably crawl into my shell, not wanting to face the world as a failure. I swallowed nervously and pulled my cosy warm blanket around me like a protective layer, until I felt a human arm around my shoulder.

"Ready for the big day Swe?" Amit asked me.

My husband had been a constant source of support especially in these last few months with regards to my training. Triathlon training wasn't a piece of cake especially with a young toddler. I watched my four-year-old daughter Samara sleeping peacefully next to me, oblivious to the air of palpable tension that I was exhibiting. I glanced at the time on my phone. It was 5:15 am. I took a deep breath as Amit patted my shoulder.

"You will be fine."

I looked at him with terror in my eyes as beads of perspiration began to form on my forehead. It felt as though I was going to war. Not exactly the term one would use to describe an Ironman 70.3 race. As much as I wanted to be in denial, the D-day was finally here – September 9th, 2018 – the day I was supposed to be swimming 1.2 miles in the ocean, bike 56 miles on rolling hills and run 13.1 miles on a trail. There were stringent cut-offs for each leg of the race. Failure to meet the cut-offs meant you were pulled off course and given an official DNF (did not finish).

Just that very thought, made me shudder! I then recollected the cut-off time for each leg.

1.2 mile swim – One hour and ten minutes. I had to finish my swim within this time frame to qualify for the next stage which was Transition 1.

Transition 1: The swim to bike transition usually took the longest, going by my previous experience at other triathlon events. From the beach, it was about 0.3 miles to Depot Park, the transition point where the bikes were racked. Getting off the wetsuit was a mammoth task. It clung to you like a second skin. Besides that, you are cold and exhausted from the swim. The longer time spent in this transition meant that you had less time to meet the bike cut-off. The total cut-off for the swim, Transition 1 and bike was five hours and thirty minutes.

For instance, if I took one hour for my swim and ten minutes at Transition 1, then I just had four hours and twenty minutes to finish the 56 miles bike ride. Considering that the bike course at Santa Cruz was hilly with 2000 feet elevation gain, coupled with headwinds, it is always better to finish a quick swim and spend as little time as possible in Transition 1. The question was, would I be able to manage it?

56 miles biking – Five hours and thirty minutes to finish the swim, Transition 1 plus bike portion.

Transition 2: The transition from the bike to run is also tough, considering your legs feel wobbly after biking for a long time. If you do meet the cut-offs, then it is always advisable to spend less time in Transition 2 which will give you more time on the run. After biking, it takes at least two miles to get your rhythm in running.

13.1 mile run – The entire race including the swim, bike and run has to be completed in eight hours and thirty minutes. So, if you finish your swim in one hour, take ten minutes at Transition 1 and four hours and ten minutes on the bike, then you have three hours and ten minutes to finish your 13.1 mile run.

Every athlete had to finish the race in eight and a half hours to be eligible for the finisher's medal.

Could I really do it?

In the past, I had envisioned crossing the finish line holding the country flag in my hands. I closed my eyes and tried to visualize this scene again. In my dream, I saw myself filled with a feeling of elation, of having earned the title of the Ironman. An achievement that I thought was beyond my reach. I saw the happy faces of my husband and daughter, the accolades I would receive from my running community and finally the glee of having attained a sense of worth.

I stood up feeling slightly giddy, trying to grapple the million thoughts swarming my head. The positive vision was replaced by this sudden dark force, pummelling my head with another set of contradictory thoughts.

What if I don't make the swim cut-off? What if I got tired in the middle of the swim? What if the ocean currents threw me off course? I had heard that even the most seasoned athletes sometimes failed to make the swim cut-offs. That made me even more nervous. It would be such a blow to be hauled out of the water and asked to go home. I imagined myself getting pulled out of the water while I watched the other athletes hurry towards the transition point to mount on their bikes. I would be a loser. I shook my head. No. This cannot happen. I sat down again feeling weak. My breath was rapid and my stomach curled itself into those nervous knots.

"Are you okay Swe?" Amit asked.

"Will I be considered a loser if I don't make the cut-offs? I mean, what if I don't and what if this turns out to be a waste of your time and money? Will you think I am good for nothing? What will Viv feel? I am scared."

Viv was my coach who had religiously been giving me a triathlon training plan for a year. He had more faith in my abilities than I did as he encouraged me to do the Ironman 70.3 race. Even though I had done a few triathlon events in the last one year, I still felt those bouts of nervousness. These had been much shorter distances like the Sprint and Olympic distances. The Sprint distance comprised of 0.45 miles swimming, 12.5 miles biking and 3.1 miles running. The Olympic distance involved 0.95 miles swimming, 25 miles biking and 6.2 miles running. At these events, there were no cut-off times for the swim.

Since there were no cut-off timings, I would often take my own sweet time wading through the waves. I usually swam with my head up as the chilling waters would make me shiver and lose my breath easily. I was instructed numerous times by Coach Jay of PacWest Endurance to put my head down while swimming, at his swim clinics.

"You will swim faster if your body is more vertically positioned. When your head is up, your legs weigh you down and that would cause a lot of fatigue," he said.

What if I am unable to put my head down today? What if I end up panicking and choking in the middle of my swim? The ocean could be temperamental and capricious. Sighting the marker buoys was challenging with the waves and currents. One could easily drift away. Besides there were sea lions present around the wharf. What if they came near me? I trembled just at the mere thought.

"Swe, you will definitely make the cut-offs. I know your strength. You are underestimating yourself. Nobody is going to think low of you," Amit reassured me.

His voice was drowned by another wave of thoughts that swarmed in my head like a hurricane.

I wish I had been exposed to open water swimming from childhood. Unfortunately, ocean swimming was not so common back in India as compared to the western countries. Besides, due to my fear of water, I did not learn to swim until the age of eleven. Now, swimming in a pool seemed like soaking in a bathtub as compared to swimming in the ocean. Did I make a mistake jumping into the Ironman 70.3 journey too soon? It was just a year since I started my triathlon journey in California. Was I really ready for it? The ugly heads of self-doubt began to raise their head. I knew that this was not the best time to harbour such negative thoughts. But I couldn't help it.

Across from my room at the Ocean Pacific Lodge in Santa Cruz, I could see Depot Park from the window. This was the transition area where the athletes had parked their bikes a day before the event. It was scheduled to open at 5:00 am and I could already see a few participants streaming in. Amit urged me to get up and get ready.

"Relax Swe. Remember what you told me when you signed up for this race? You said that in case you failed to make the cut-offs, you will take it as a learning experience and come back stronger next year. No matter what happens today, you will always be a winner to me."

"Hmm okay!"

"Come on. Cheer up. You will feel much better when you go out there and talk to a few people."

I gathered my things and did a quick check list in my transition bag.

- Towel. A purple one that I had used in all my other triathlon events. Check.

- A white plastic bag. To dump my dripping wetsuit post swimming. Check.
- Wetsuit. A pretty pink and grey one that elicited admiring looks from other triathletes. Check.
- Swim cap. A pink one given at the Ironman Expo a day before, it matched my wetsuit. Check.
- Body glide. Made it easier to slip on my wetsuit. Check.
- Two pairs of swim goggles. As advised by Coach Jay in case a strap of one broke. Check.
- Ear plugs. As advised by Penni at my first swim clinic. Check.
- Helmet. My protective crowning glory against the much-dreaded accidents. Check.
- Bike glasses. Roka brand glasses that I got from the Santa Rosa Ironman Expo. Check.
- Gatorade bottles. My fuel during races. Check.
- Running shoes. Pink in colour with multicolour laces. Check.
- Vizar cap. It read Ironman and I sincerely wished my dream would come true. Check.
- Energy gels also known as Gu gels. Strawberry and banana flavour, my favourite. Check.
- Fuel belt. One that I tied around my waist and carried all those energy Gu gels. Check.
- Cliff bars. For further fuelling in case I felt hungry during the course. Check.

- Garmin watch. To help me keep track of my pace and time, thankfully it was charged 100 per cent. Check.
- Timing chip. Boy! I wouldn't forget this one after what happened in my very first triathlon. Incidentally it was at this same place. Check.

I seemed to have everything that was required for the race. I put on my black and green tri-suit that read Ironman. I had recently got this one. I quickly tied my hair into a ponytail. I took a couple of nervous bites from the peanut butter sandwich that Amit had prepared. Unable to eat anymore, I shoved it in his hands.

"Swe, you will feel hungry. Please eat something."

I shook my head. As I headed towards the door, I paused for a minute and turned.

"Amit? If I do manage to make the swim and the bike cut-offs, I am sure I will finish the race. Having been a runner for the last six years, I think I will finish the run portion in a strong manner. In that case, will you please bring the Indian flag and wait for me just a few yards before the finish line? The finish is at the beach so wait for me on West Cliff Drive. I will collect the flag from you and cross the Ironman 70.3 finish line holding my country's flag."

"Good luck. You are definitely going to make it," he said.

I then walked out of the room, took a right and down

towards the corridor into the entrance area, carrying my bag consisting of my triathlon kit. It was a rather cold morning and I had my jacket on. It was still dark but Depot Park was lit up as though it was Christmas. I had to just cross the road to enter the transition area. There was a long line of athletes, waiting to check into transition. Their families stood around, chattering away happily. I scanned the confident faces around me listening to their incessant rant about getting a PR (personal record). PR is when an athlete beats his/her timing from a previous race. It is a proud moment as it showcases their fitness and hard work that they have put in. It further emphasizes the saying that you ultimately compete with yourself and you have to focus on bettering yourself than beating others. A philosophy that I usually follow.

"Hey, be sure to click me near the finish line," one man was telling his wife. "I hope to get a PR on my bike," said another lady to her friend. The athletes were a sturdy lot who looked as though they had been training for years. I felt like a kid in front of them. After all, I was a novice. How I longed to be like them – folks who appeared as though they could wake up and just do a 70.3 race. While here I was, not even sure of crossing the first hurdle.

How I wish I could make my family proud today. I recollected Samara's words that she had randomly uttered the day before at lunch, "Mama you are a champion!"

My eyes suddenly filled with tears at the thought of disappointing my family.

At the entrance of the holding area, I displayed my green wrist band which said Ironman 70.3. It was given to all participants the day before at the Ironman Village, where athletes had to pick up their bib numbers, swim caps, T-shirts and timing chips. Without the wrist band, athletes would be barred from entering the holding area.

"You are good to go," said the security official.

I entered the area and went straight to the spot where I had racked my bike the previous day. It was assigned by participants' bib numbers. I found mine which read 624. Rocky – my white Felt brand road bike was a little moist due to the morning dew. I looked at my bike fondly. It had seen me through several triathlon events and all my training rides. It had stood rock solid by me. I prayed and hoped that it wouldn't let me down today. A bike was a triathlete's best friend, at least in my opinion.

I checked the pressure on both the tyres to see if they had sufficient air. I noticed another participant on my left filling air with his pump. I meekly asked him to check if my tyres needed more air. He felt them gingerly.

"They are good to go," he said.

"Cool. Thanks!" I muttered gratefully.

Another fear that nagged me constantly was the possibility of getting a flat tyre in the middle of the race. I sighed thinking how running was a simpler sport in comparison to a triathlon. In running, you sort of had control over your outcome if you took care of your hydration and nutrition. At least you didn't have to battle ocean currents, sea lions or worry about getting a flat tyre.

It was 6:15 am and I looked around. The smell of morning dew wafted into my nostrils. Athletes were busy adjusting their bikes, laying down their things on the towel or engaging in a friendly banter with their groups. Some of them looked solemn and dead serious which made me feel even more nervous. While others seemed relaxed and easygoing as though they had come to enjoy a picnic. I wished I could adopt the latter approach but it seemed impossible to do so, considering my turbulent mind.

I set my towel on the ground. I began to place my things on it in the order of swim, bike and run. Out came the pink swim cap, two pairs of swim goggles, ear plugs and body glide. I placed my helmet on the bike and racked the Gatorade bottles along the stem of the bike. I pasted a bib around the stem of my bike and placed my running bib, running shoes and another bottle of Gatorade on the towel. Besides that, I kept my fuel belt that held my Gu gels and energy bars.

I noticed a middle-aged athletic lady towards my right. She was setting up her stuff as well. Our eyes met and we exchanged a smile.

"Your first time?" I asked.

"No, actually I did this last year," she said. "What about you?"

"My first time."

"Oh, you are going to be fine. It looks like a great day."

I looked up to see that the sun was beginning to come out. I was relieved that it wasn't a foggy morning. The ocean wouldn't be very cold in that case, which would make my swim easier. Just the previous week, I had a tough time putting my face into the cold water. It felt as though someone had depleted oxygen from my lungs as I was left gasping and spluttering.

The transition area emanated positive vibes. The darkness gave way to a bright sunny morning. The blue sky hung about like a painting above us as the sun shone brightly, almost as though it was smiling at us. Cheerful looking volunteers walked by to ensure all the participants were body marked. Body marking was mandatory for all athletes where the bib number was written with a dark sketch pen on the left arm while the age was written on the left calf.

"Body marking? Body marking?" they went around calling out to the athletes. One of them stopped next to a bike on my left.

A kind faced man was getting his age marked on his left calf. When the volunteer asked his age, the man replied 45. For some reason, the volunteer heard it as 55

13

and the man exclaimed in mock horror. "Oh no, you don't wanna make me so old already," he chuckled and looked at me, including me in the joke.

I smiled, feeling much better than I did earlier that morning. I held my arm during my turn while a nice lady marked me with her black sketch pen.

"There you go. You are all set. Good luck."

"Thanks!" I replied, "I badly need it."

"Oh, you are going to be fine."

After the body marking, I applied body glide all over my arms, legs and neck. This would make it easier to slip on my stiff wetsuit over my tri-suit. I put on my pink swim cap and adjusted the swim goggles on top of my cap. I strapped my timing chip on my left ankle. I headed down to Cowell Beach which was about 0.3 miles away. The start line of Ironman 70.3 Santa Cruz was right on the beach.

While walking towards the sands, I acquainted myself with another lady.

"It's my first time," she mentioned.

"Oh, mine too," I exclaimed.

"Oh cool. We are on the same boat. I am so nervous."

I nodded understandingly.

"My family is here to cheer for me. If I make the cut-offs, great. You never know if you can do it unless you try, right?" she said cheerfully.

I admired her spirit.

"Good luck to you. Hope you make it," I said sincerely.

"Thanks. To you too!" she smiled.

The beach looked quite picturesque with its turquoise blue waters. How I wish I was on a vacation instead of this gruelling race. The sands were swarming with athletes in wetsuits. I saw the arch that read Ironman 70.3. It was the finish line and for the millionth time I wished I could cross it later that afternoon. There was still 20 minutes for the race to start. So, some of the participants used this time to warm up in the ocean. With the sun already up, the water looked warm and inviting. The yellow and orange buoys bobbed on the blue mass of waves. What a pretty sight! I thought. I saw some athletes come out of the water.

"How's the water?" I asked.

"Oh, pretty good. Not so cold today."

My heart did a little jig of relief.

I decided to do some warm up laps as well. This was highly recommended before any swim or a triathlon event. I edged closer to the ocean. Taking one step at a time, I gradually entered the waves. They came bouncing up to my hip. 'Welcome', they seemed to say, gradually pulling me in. I closed my eyes and slowly put my face in the water. Memories of my first open water swim came flooding back to me. I could still reminisce that day when I landed here for my first open water swim. I also recollected the reasons as to why I decided to venture into the triathlon journey in the first place. And why doing the Ironman 70.3 race was important to me.

Cowell Beach at Santa Cruz was the same place where I had attended my first open water swim clinic a year ago – August 5th, 2017. Incidentally I did my very first triathlon at this same place. Now I was doing my Ironman 70.3. Life sure does come a full circle, I thought.

The experience was still so vivid in my mind….

Chapter 2

Facing the Summer Blues

"There is a light at the end of every tunnel."

– Ada Adams

I had landed in the Bay area on June 28th. It was just a day after my birthday. Not exactly the birthday present that I would have ideally liked.

Heavily jet lagged, I was shown into our accommodation inside the Stanford Campus. It resembled a cosy cottage and was semi-furnished. The living room and kitchen were adjacent to one another. There was a sliding door that opened into our patio and overlooked a courtyard. Surrounding the courtyard were a row of houses. There was also a play area for children. The lawns were perfectly manicured and it appeared as though someone had spread a green carpet. The image was almost surreal and I couldn't imagine anything looking so perfect.

A month had elapsed and before I realized, it was

August already. I sat on the sofa in my living room and gazed out of the window. Being summer, the weather was just perfect. It was bright and sunny. Squeals of laughter floated from the courtyard. I spotted a few squirrels jumping on to the branches of the trees from the wall of my patio. The sound of birds echoed along the yard, making it seem as though they were a part of an orchestra. The entire scenario appeared right out of a Disney animation.

I was in Stanford! One of the best universities in the world with top-class amenities. I knew several people who would do anything just to be here. So, why was I not as elated as I should have been? Why did it feel like my mind was engulfed by this thick black fog? As sunny as it was outdoors, I felt as though I was wrapped up in a blanket of gloom. I couldn't get myself to eat or drink properly. I went about the household chores like a zombie and responded in mono syllables to Amit and Samara.

Amit was enrolled in a one year programme at the Graduate School of Business and his classes had already begun. Samara was at her day care. I was enrolled in creative writing classes as well, at the continuing studies programme. However, I couldn't help feeling this big void. Like something important had been taken away from my life.

Back in India, I was always on the move, especially living in Mumbai that was often cited as the New York of the East. Working as a journalist for a business website, I was in-charge of the literary section. I was required to keep tab of the latest books, attend book launches and interview authors. I was on the mailing list of many publishing houses and was constantly getting invites or interview requests for several of their book releases. In short, I felt a sense of importance and had an identity of my own.

Running being a passion, my husband and I were a part of this large running community called Mumbai Road Runners that comprised of more than 10,000 runners. Every first Sunday of the month, most of us would meet for a 13 mile run which would usually end with a breakfast at one of those joints that served toast and eggs. Considering there were several such events every other Sunday, our weekends would be packed just meeting our runner friends.

This lively and effervescent community left us with no room for loneliness back home. Their absence was now beginning to feel quite conspicuous to me in the Bay area within just a month's time. Especially since I couldn't find a similar community here. Being a runner and a journalist, I felt close to nothing else. It seemed as though my identity had suddenly been snatched away. I had to start from scratch again – something that I wasn't looking forward to. I wondered if it was actually worth getting out my comfort zone.

I still remember the day when Amit joyfully remarked that he had secured admission at the Stanford Business School. One fine April morning, he woke me up from my sleep. I looked at his excited face that resembled that of a kid in a candy store.

"What's up?" I mumbled snuggling inside my blanket.

"Swe, I got it!" he said excitedly.

"Got what?"

"Admission at Stanford. They just sent me an email. Look!" he thrust his phone into my hands.

I rubbed my eyes, glanced at it and then looked at his elated face.

Knots began to form in my stomach and a wave of dread washed over me like a tsunami. Suddenly I felt my world come crashing down. I wanted to feel happy for him but deep down I felt a large vacuum at the thought of leaving my beloved city. I had a lot of support in terms of domestic help to do the household chores, family support and a trusted preschool-cum-day care to take care of my daughter while I was at work. I knew that there was no such help in the US – one of the reasons I never wanted to live abroad.

I forced myself to smile at him and mumbled, "Congrats!" What a horrible person I had suddenly become, I thought to myself as I couldn't get myself to share his happiness.

"It is just for a year," Amit pressed, sensing my

thoughts. "Samara will be in day care and you will have an opportunity to pursue your writing classes – something that you always wanted to explore. Of course, you can still participate in running events. I am sure there will be plenty in the Bay area."

We had a detailed discussion on this when he decided to apply. I agreed half-heartedly, deciding to take this as an experience. With a heavy heart, I left my vibrant life behind and moved to California on June 28th, 2017. The first few days were spent in settling down and getting used to the new place.

Stanford Campus was huge and couldn't be explored only on foot. In order to commute to my classes and the fitness centre within the campus, I definitely needed a bike. I observed a lot of people on their bikes inside the campus and also within the city of Palo Alto. Apparently, it was a bike friendly place. So, the first thing that we did was to get ourselves bikes. I wanted to invest in a good bike and thought it would be a good idea to incorporate biking into my fitness routine as well along with my swimming, gym and running. I had no idea about bikes so I decided to speak to my friend Viv who eventually became my coach. Viv was a certified Ironman coach and an expert on bikes. I talked to him one day.

"Hey Viv, I am considering getting a bike to commute around Stanford. Any recommendations what kind of bike should I get?

"Is the bike only for short commute or are you planning on longer rides?"

"Well I do plan on incorporating biking as a part of my fitness regime. So yes, I will be doing long distance rides. I have seen a lot of bikers, the area around Stanford looks to be a haven for biking."

"Got it. Since you are planning on riding long distances, I suggest that you go for a good quality endurance bike."

"Endurance bike?"

"Okay so you need to consider three things before investing in a good bike. First, you have to look at a bike's geometry which is different for racing or endurance. Race bikes have aero geometry and are fast but uncomfortable for longer distances. Endurance road bikes offer better comfort and since it's your first bike, this will be a good choice for you. Second, is the group set or the mechanical parts of the bike – the break levers, crank, chain rings, gear shifters, etc. Shimano is a leader in this space and you should definitely look at the Shimano 105 group set or a higher priced Shimano Ultegra group set. Third, having a carbon alloy frame will be better than aluminium frames. It will be lighter and will absorb more shock in bumpy rides. And once you finalize based on these parameters, you look for the one that is around your budget and also get your bike fitted based on your height and reach."

I quickly made a note of it on my pad and asked him to repeat a few things. He did it patiently. There was certainly a lot to consider as far as investing in a bike was concerned.

"Alright! I have noted down your points carefully. Thank you so much Viv. Really appreciate it."

After I got off the call with Viv, I browsed for bike stores around the area. There was a store called Bike Connections which was located close to the Stanford Campus. Keeping Viv's advice in mind, I explored a few bikes before I settled in for a white Felt brand road bike. It fitted in well with the requirements and was also within my budget – $2300. It was an endurance bike with a carbon alloy frame and a Shimano 105 group set. When I took it for a trial ride, it felt perfect and comfortable as though I had been riding the bike for years. I purchased a helmet and a pair of gloves along with it. Amit got a black colour Giant road bike. The bike helped me explore the Stanford Campus and also commute to the fitness centre and the pool.

I began to set into a regular routine. Amit would leave by 7:30 for his classes. I would prepare the food, get Samara ready and drop her at the day care centre by 9:30. After that I would either head to the gym for a run on the treadmill or do few strength training exercises. On some days, I would go to the pool and swim 1-1.2 miles. Other days I would just take my bike out for a 15-20 mile ride on the Foothill Expressway which was 2.5 miles from my campus accommodation. Then I would work on my creative writing course assignments which involved both reading and writing. My classes were once a week in the evenings and so Amit would pick up Samara from the day care on those days.

Despite this busy schedule and routine, the much dreaded yet inevitable homesickness began to creep in. Back in India I was used to training with Amit. Training alone was no fun and I hadn't found a community yet.

I glanced at the clock on the wall. It was 12:00 noon and lunch time. I sighed and went back to my thoughts as I couldn't get myself to eat anything despite a hard workout that morning. The emptiness that I felt couldn't even be cured with a bowl of lentils and vegetables. Since childhood, this comfort food usually helped in lifting my spirits, every time I was down in the dumps. It was different today. Moodily I gazed out of the window. A few children were playing on the swings while their mothers watched them. The mothers were engaged in a lively chatter with one another which made me feel even worse as I still hadn't made any friends.

Technically I was part of the partners' community at the Graduate School of Business. The cohort organized several social dos which involved late nights and parties. Unfortunately, this wasn't my idea of fun. I had outgrown those partying days in my 20s. Being in the late 30s, I preferred meeting over coffee and quiet dinners. I also enjoyed reading and indulging in outdoor activities like running, biking or swimming in a pool. Or I would watch a movie or sports on television. I certainly didn't enjoy cooking, shopping or partying which seemed to be some of the interests of the people that I had come across so far in the community. I suppose the older you grow, the tougher it is to make friends, especially when you are the kind who seeks more meaningful relationships.

Initially I did go for a couple of those social dos with an open mind, thinking that it was a good way to get acquainted with a few people. I realized that I was bored to death and felt lost amidst the loud narcissist cacophony. For some reason, the vibes that emanated from some of the individuals here were not friendly or genuine. They appeared to be a frivolous group of people who were likely to associate themselves with you only if you were well connected in the Bay area. Way different from the selfless and genuine community that I was accustomed to back in Mumbai city.

Hosting dinner at my place for the Indian members of the cohort didn't help either. As a host, they failed to acknowledge me and chose to mingle with the rest of the guests instead. For the first time in several years, I felt like an outcast in my own house and at my own party. I was particularly miffed at the lack of etiquette shown by some of them. Leaving abruptly without even offering to help in clean up or thanking the hosts for a party was enough to make me withdraw into my shell. Just a month back at my farewell party in India, my runner friends stayed right till the end and helped us clean up the entire place. My dislike for the business school community further enhanced when some of the Indians who weren't invited began to send out nasty emails and indulged in a blame game.

Though my husband agreed and empathized with my thoughts, he chose to shrug it off with a statement saying, "There are all kinds of people in this world."

"True," I retorted, "just that I don't have to put up with them."

However, after these few instances, I couldn't help feeling a slight dent in my self-confidence, wondering if there was something wrong with me. From then on, I decided to focus on finding more meaningful things such as my running and my workouts which gave me a sense of accomplishment. Something to make me feel, that fitting in at the business school community wasn't the only way one could earn respect.

As a start, I had already participated in the San Francisco Half Marathon on July 23rd, which was just 10 days ago. It was my first event in California. However, it wasn't enough to keep me riding on a high. I wanted something more.

Just then the key to the lock turned and I jumped at the sound of the door open.

"Hi Swe," Amit called out.

"Aren't you supposed to be in class?" I asked puzzled.

"We got an hour off for lunch so I thought I'll come and check on you. Have you had lunch?"

I shook my head, suddenly feeling my eyes sting with tears.

"Are you okay?" Amit came and sat down next to me on the sofa.

The merry laughter of the children continued to float from the courtyard along with the gentle summer breeze.

"I... I... I am feeling so out of place here. I wish I hadn't come. I have tried but I don't seem to fit in here. Back in Mumbai, I was treated with so much respect. I feel so incompetent here."

"Swe you just ran a half marathon within three and a half weeks of coming here. That's simply amazing. Give yourself a break. Besides you also have your classes."

"Easy for you to speak. You have everything going for you. Don't you understand? I don't want to be known as just another partner here. I don't want to be known just as your wife or Samara's mother. I want to establish an identity of my own. Doing the household chores by myself is driving me nuts. I can't seem to find friends. I want something beyond these chores, my running and writing. I want to do something that will give me a sense of achievement," I paused feeling my face go hot and redden. My breathing was fast and rapid. My hands were shaking.

27

Amit looked at me with worry and instantly handed over a glass of water. I drank it and continued staring at the window listlessly. All of a sudden, he turned to me with a sparkle in his eyes like he had stumbled upon something big.

"Swe!" he said excitedly.

"What?"

"Remember how you said you wanted to try your hand at triathlons? You have been saying that when you were in India and were also planning to do one in the city of Hyderabad in October. Why don't you participate in some triathlon events here?"

"The swimming at the Hyderabad event was to be held in a swimming pool. Are there any triathlon events held here where swims are in a pool? Well I don't mind. You know I can't swim in the ocean or a lake."

Amit grabbed my laptop that was lying in front of me and began to surf vigorously. After about 30 minutes he nudged me.

"Look I came across a few events in the Bay area. Most of the events are conducted in open waters. However, I have looked at few swim clinics where coaches help first timers get acclimatized to open waters. I think you should give it a shot," he said.

"There are sessions for first timers?" I asked. For the first time in several days, I saw a faint glimmer of hope.

"Yes, check out this page. It is an event called Tri Santa

Cruz. I've mailed it to you. I'll quickly grab a bite and run for class. Will see you in the evening?"

I didn't respond as I scanned my email and clicked on the link on my iPhone. My eyes were transfixed on the details of the event page. The swim clinic was for just one day which was on August 5th, 2017 – this coming Saturday. It clearly said that this open water swim clinic was for first timers and they'd teach us both the open water and transition skills for a triathlon. It was to be held only for one day.

Amidst all this chaos, I had almost forgotten my dream that I had been harbouring in India. I had planned on doing a triathlon sometime in October, but somehow it got shelved due to the big move.

I was a decent swimmer in the pool and could swim comfortably for an hour. I was also riding my bike regularly ever since I got to Stanford. I wondered how it would be to swim in the ocean. Well, I'd find out this Saturday. I signed up for the swim clinic and began to watch few videos of triathletes. How deftly they swam their strokes in the open water. They seem so poised and at ease.

As I closed my eyes, I visualized myself swimming in the ocean, biking and running to cross the finish line. To be known as a triathlete would be a dream come true. Something that would challenge me beyond running. Not to mention, it would give me a sense of accomplishment and a new identity. Hopefully it would also restore my sense of worth and self-confidence. Maybe training for it would take my mind off about being incompetent and not worrying about making friends.

As the clock ticked away seconds, I had already begun counting time for my first swim clinic. It was at Cowell Beach in a place called Santa Cruz. I suddenly began to feel better as I had something to look forward to. Little did I realize that my first open water swim was an event that I'd remember till my last breath....

Chapter 3

Braving the Tsunami of Fears on Cowell Beach

"Water your ambitions, burn your inhibitions."
– Mahathi Anand

It wasn't exactly love at first sight with Cowell Beach.

Situated on the west of the Municipal wharf in downtown Santa Cruz, it was roughly an hour from Stanford Campus. Cowell Beach was popular for volleyball and surfing. The Santa Cruz Beach Boardwalk – an amusement park, located five minutes from the beach, was frequented by families on weekends. After reading the reviews online, there was a certain image that was etched in my mind. A sun kissed beach with pristine blue water and folks indulging in a friendly game of volleyball.

I was a little taken aback when I landed there for the first time. It was a foggy morning and the entire beach looked as though someone had draped a grey sheet over it.

I could almost taste the mist in my mouth while I gaped at the morbid atmosphere around me. The ocean looked grey, intimidating and cold.

Amit and Samara too accompanied me to my first swim clinic that was conducted by Finish Line Productions – an event management company that organized running events and triathlons. As instructed in the email, participants were asked to assemble near Lifeguard Tower 1 at Cowell Beach at 8:00 am. The GPS directed us to this location. Surprisingly, the beach looked deserted. My family and I stood there surveying the sands. Surely there would have been at least a few registrants for the clinic?

"Amit, I hope we aren't at the wrong place," I said nervously.

"Relax. Let's wait for a bit and see," Amit reassured me.

"Boy! This isn't what I expected. The water looks so cold! I don't think I have the guts to get in."

"Chill Swe. Worst case scenario, if you can't make it, we will just have a good time at the beach, hang out here until lunch and go home."

"Okay!"

"Now come on, let's go down to the beach and try to find someone."

There were a series of steps that led to the sands. Clutching my bag, we climbed down and walked around, hoping to spot someone. We soon caught sight of a wetsuit rental shop with a man seated on a chair, writing down something on a notebook. I walked up to him.

"Hello. Would you happen to know where Lifeguard Tower 1 is?"

He looked up.

"Oh hey. Yes sure. Its right over there," he said pointing to a tower just a few yards away from us.

"Thanks. I was actually here for a swim clinic and the mail instructed us to meet at Lifeguard Tower 1."

"Well that is the place. Probably they are running late."

"Okay!"

"So where are you from?"

"From India, but we are currently living in Stanford."

"Nice. Are you studying there?"

"Yes, my husband is doing a one year programme at the Graduate School of Business. I am pursing some courses in creative writing."

Just at that moment, Amit and Samara came up.

"Hi, Amit here," he said extending his hand with a smile.

"I am Jake," said the man.

"And I am Swetha. So how cold is the water?" I asked darting a nervous look at the ocean. A few seagulls swooped down the sands and began to pick on something.

"Well depends. I would say it is really cold. About 50 degrees Fahrenheit. But if you have wetsuits on, you should be fine."

"What are those seagulls pecking on?"

"Must be some tiny crabs or dead fish."

"Crabs?" I asked nervously.

For some inexplicable reason since my childhood, I was petrified of those multiple-legged creatures that moved sideways. I recollected an incident back on a beach in India. I was standing at the shore, enjoying the feel of the waves brushing against my legs. That image of a large white crab on my feet after the waves retreated, still sends shivers down my spine. I shrieked so loudly that I embarrassed my mother who had turned red at the onlookers' curious glances towards my direction.

"Hmm, do the crabs come out?"

"Swe come on," my husband interrupted.

"Oh, don't worry about it. They are usually buried below the sands," said Jake.

"I don't think I can go through it. I mean I am not used to cold water," I said pulling my jacket closer. "And those crabs…."

"Oh, you don't have to worry about them. They never come out," Jake assured me.

"I am not used to swimming in cold water especially not open waters. My pool was always heated even during winters."

"I see," he said throwing me a sympathetic glance. "Well, you never know until you really go for it and see what it's like. At least you know you had the courage to try it once."

"Hmm, okay!"

"Oh, look there they come."

I looked up to see some people coming down the steps carrying their bags. Probably containing wetsuits, swim goggles and a towel just like mine. They soon assembled near the Lifeguard Tower.

After saying goodbye to Jake, I walked towards the crowd. I spotted a group of Indians and looked at them with interest. For some reason, their presence gave me some reassurance. I then noticed a strong woman standing in the centre and taking charge. She had a round face, an athletic build and short hair. She introduced herself as Penni and asked us to sit in a circle. She talked about her triathlon journey and mentioned how she had completed a few Ironman distances – that included 2.4 miles swimming, 112 miles biking and 26.2 miles running. I looked at her in awe.

There was an initial round of introductions from which I gathered information about the Indian group. They were part of Team Asha – a non-profit group that raises funds for the education of the underprivileged. Rajeev Char, as he introduced himself was their coach. After the introductory round, Penni looked at us and asked.

"So, how many first timers here?"

I was relieved to see a few other people raise their hands as well.

"I would like each of you to share your inhibitions about open water swimming," said Penni.

As the responses began to come in, I discovered that most people feared sharks and drowning.

When it came to my turn, I replied meekly "The cold temperature and the currents." The thought of sharks hadn't occurred to me until then. Now there was one more thing to worry about.

"Alright. So, let us address one fear at a time," Penni said briskly. "First of all, there is a healthy population of sea lions around the wharf. So that rules out the presence of a predator. Secondly, you guys will be wearing your wetsuits that are designed to make you stay afloat. There is no way you can drown with a wetsuit. They will keep you warm as well."

"Now," she continued, "start putting on your wetsuits. We will get into the water and do some warm up strokes first. Once all of you are comfortable, we will swim up to that buoy that you see over there," she said pointing to a yellow colour one at a distance. "Rob here will be on his kayak. If you are feeling uncomfortable, just raise your hand and he will be with you in a jiffy."

A sturdy looking man with a cheerful face waved at us with his paddle.

"Before you put on your wetsuits, there are a couple of things that you need to keep in mind," Penni continued, "I highly recommend the use of body glide." She held a tube of a lubricant in her hands. "You need to apply this all over your body before you get into your wetsuit so that it becomes easier to slip in and slip out of your suit. I also recommend using earplugs to avoid the possibilities of an ear infection that could come from swimming in open waters."

Oh dear! So many things to keep in mind, I thought.

Shaking slightly, I opened my bag and took out my wetsuit. It was a black suit which I used for deep sea diving. I had bought it in 2013 during my trip to Australia. It had been four years since I went diving. I recollected how petrified I was going underwater initially. I was probably more daring and adventurous back then that made it easier to conquer my fears. Something had changed after my pregnancy in 2014. My thoughts were interrupted by Penni's brisk voice.

"Hey, are you sure you will be warm in that? The water is really cold," she asked feeling my wetsuit. "You need a thicker one," she said, displaying hers as a sample.

"B... but I only have this," I panicked.

"Relax. We will see if anyone has an extra suit that you could borrow today," she reassured me.

While she went around checking, I looked on helplessly, kicking myself for not having double checked the requirements before. The rest of the participants had thick body suits identical to Penni's while mine stood out like a sore thumb. I hoped and prayed that someone would have a spare wetsuit. Tears filled my eyes and I turned my face, afraid of coming across as a baby.

I caught sight of Amit who was watching Samara build sand castles. He looked up at that moment. Seeing panic on my face, they both came over.

"What happened?" he asked concerned.

"Apparently I require a thicker wetsuit. Otherwise I will freeze in the water," I said miserably.

"Hold on. Don't panic," he pointed to Jake's wetsuit rental.

Why didn't I think of it earlier? I rushed towards the stall.

"What's up?" asked Jake.

"I actually need a thicker wetsuit. Mine doesn't match the requirements."

"Ahh yes. What you got is a thinner one and you will freeze in the ocean. I can get you a thicker one," he said looking at the racks and pulling out a dark grey suit.

"Here you go. That should fit you fine. And good luck."

"Thanks. I need it," I muttered, giving him a grateful look.

I rushed to the group.

"So, you managed to get one," Penni said. "Alright! The first timers stay with me while the rest of you can go ahead and take a few warm-up laps."

I walked towards the ocean. The waves brushed against my legs first before I let them come up to my waist. It felt as though a dozen buckets of ice were hurled upon me. I froze, refusing to take a step further.

"Come on," Penni beckoned.

Closing my eyes, I went in further and by now the water had reached my neck. I gasped and spluttered, holding on to the swimmer nearby.

"Easy," he said. "Just relax and take a deep breath."

I saw that it was Coach Char.

"I... I... ," I spluttered gasping for breath. It felt like the oxygen levels had depleted in my body.

"Just lie on your back and float," he said kindly.

I tried doing that but the temperature was too cold for me to handle. I quickly got out of the water. In the meantime others had already begun their laps.

I stood there shivering, trying to get over the sudden cold wave that hit me. I was reminded of my first swimming class when I was eleven years old. I could recollect that day even today...

"I... I... will drown," I gasped.

"I am holding you. Don't worry," my instructor coaxed me gently. He was a kind faced and a patient man who promised me I would be swimming like a fish within a month's time.

"I... I... am scared," I spluttered coughing as I accidently swallowed water after entering the pool.

"Relax. Just hold on to this float," he said, pushing a round yellow tube towards me.

I remember holding on to it and kicking my way across the pool. I watched other children float effortlessly while I was clinging on a yellow blub. I felt like the odd one out. It took me about ten days to enjoy being in water. However, it took me around three weeks to get rid of the float. Over time, my inhibitions and fears dropped along with the float. As he promised, I was swimming like a fish in four weeks and I never looked back ever since.

Until today when I stood helplessly at the mercy of the ruthless ocean feeling like that eleven-year old again, I watched others swim effortlessly.

"How are you doing," asked Penni, swimming towards me.

I shook my head miserably.

"Come with me. We will swim up to Rob," she said pointing to the kayak which was just a few metres away.

"I… I… can't…," I stammered and my teeth chattered.

"Don't worry. I will be right next to you. Come on."

I hesitantly entered the ocean again. No, it didn't feel better. I panicked and choked while Penni stood there patiently. The salty taste of the water made me feel squeamish. My body wasn't accustomed to such freezing temperatures, thinking of the warm temperature controlled water in my pool. Maybe I should just stick to pool swimming. Maybe I wasn't meant to swim in the ocean. I gave Penni an apologetic look and went back to the sands.

"What happened Swe?" Amit asked.

"I don't think I have it in me to swim in the ocean. I think I should just go home."

"Come on. Of course, you do."

"No Amit, I can't take the cold. It is freezing me to death."

"You just need to acclimatize. I know you. You are not a quitter. It's not like you. You have come this far. Just give it one more chance."

Suddenly something snapped inside. In a flash, I recollected an incident that occurred six months ago. I had a bad fall in the middle of a half marathon at a place called Auroville in South India. My knee was bleeding profusely. It was around the 10th mile. I spent around five minutes getting first aid from the volunteers. I remember how I refused to quit especially having come so far and was determined to finish the race even if it meant limping to the finish line.

"Remember how you mentioned that you wanted to achieve this dream of yours Swe?" Amit continued.

I closed my eyes for a minute and thought about how I had felt ever since I had landed in Stanford. I reflected back to the conversation that I had with Amit last week. That dinner scene with the Indian community played in my mind like a tape-recorder. I remembered the feeling of anger and resentment that I felt in my own house, the feeling of being ignored by a bunch of individuals who lacked etiquette and courtesy. I then remembered the promise I had made to myself that I too was worthy of achieving something. If I wasn't going to make friends here, I sure wouldn't drown myself in misery.

"You will be fine. Just take one step at a time," Penni interrupted my thoughts, as she came up to me.

I held her hand and walked towards the ocean with great trepidation. I was shivering. How I longed for a warm blanket and hot chocolate. I told myself repeatedly that this initial bout of discomfort would prove beneficial in the long run. It was ultimately for a dream that I had nurtured for months, especially ever since I saw a triathlon video of athletes in wetsuits who got into the water so effortlessly.

Maybe this is just one of those stepping stones to success. Maybe the day when I cross the finish line of a triathlon, all this effort would be worth it. After all a caterpillar also goes through a struggle before it becomes a beautiful butterfly.

As I moved closer to the waves, I felt a surge of panic, as though I was being led to the gallows.

"Come on. Just relax. I am here with you," said Penni as though she had read my thoughts.

Taking a deep breath, I entered the water again....

Chapter 4

Transitioning into A New Skill

"Never give up! Failure and rejection
are the first steps to succeeding."

– Jim Valvano

I cautiously took one step at a time, letting the waves circle me slowly. For every step that I took, Penni gave me a pat on my shoulder. As I went deeper into the ocean, I held Penni's hand and took a deep breath as instructed by her. When the water reached up to my neck, I began swimming with breast strokes. This particular stroke required me to keep my head up so I slowly began to feel comfortable. Penni made me swim a few yards before taking me back to the shore.

"How do you feel?" she asked.

"Slightly better."

"You are doing good. The water is pretty cold. It takes a while to warm up in the ocean. After that you will be fine."

In the meantime, the others had come out of the water and assembled near Penni.

"How do you all feel?"

A couple of newcomers had few queries as they came towards her.

"We can do another round of laps," she said.

We gathered around Penni who led the way.

Taking a deep breath, I entered the waters. It wasn't so bad this time. Penni was right. It was just a matter of getting used to it.

Initially I began with breast strokes and then shifted to freestyle. This was my usual routine in the pool as well. The only difference being that I kept my head up while swimming free style. I knew it wasn't the right technique but I couldn't help it. The thought of putting my head in the freezing water and being unable to see anything below petrified me. It felt like I was almost blind, unlike in the pool where I was treated to the sight of turquoise blue waters and the floor. I was also scared of drifting away in the ocean.

"You are doing fine. We should work on putting your head down when you swim," Penni remarked as she came over to me.

I nodded half-heartedly hoping she wouldn't persist. Thankfully her attention was diverted to another new swimmer.

I slowly began to enjoy the feel of being amidst the

waves as I bobbed up and down. Once I got used to the cold, it wasn't so bad. While swimming back to the shore, I felt the waves giving me a gentle push. I felt myself gliding back to the sands. Amit and Samara were waiting for me.

"How did it go?" he asked.

"Better. Much better," I replied.

"Good."

"Planning to go in again?"

"Hmm... should I?" I said while glancing at the ocean. Just then my group headed by Penni came by.

"How do you feel?" she asked.

"Better," I said.

"Great. We thought we will just swim up to that point over there, pointing to a buoy. Rob will come with us and we will have two experienced swimmers from Team Asha to watch out for us."

"Hmm I can't," I said feeling that surge of panic rush through my veins.

"Don't worry. You will be fine."

"Go for it Swe," Amit goaded me. "Remember your goal."

I once again entered the waters. I guess my body had gotten accustomed to the temperature or probably the wetsuit was finally doing its job. I swam slowly, still keeping my head up. The waves seem to churn, making me want to puke but I held my head high, literally speaking. Coach Char was there encouraging us. There were times when the waves intimidated me as I went deeper. I looked behind and saw how far we had come from the shore.

I suddenly psyched out. Goodness, I thought. What if I am unable to swim back to the shore? I felt the blood pulsating through my veins and those knots in my stomach. I glanced at the swimmers near me who were slowly swimming their laps. My breathing became heavy due to the sudden panic. I gasped.

"You are doing great. Keep going," Coach Char encouraged me. "You are almost there," he said, pointing to the buoy.

Feeling motivated, I swam up to the buoy. I smiled at the other swimmers who had gathered around the buoy, catching their breaths. It was a comforting feeling to know that we were all in this together.

"Look at you. You are smiling now," remarked Coach Char. I gave him a grateful look. He apparently was a wonderful coach – patient and encouraging. How I wished I could join his group.

After waiting for a few minutes to catch my breath, I geared up to swim back towards the shore. Somehow being stationary at one place in the ocean made me feel giddy. It was probably the effect of the salt content. I felt better when I was moving. I began to swim back to the shore. It was easier this time as the waves gently pushed me. It appeared as though they were my ally in this journey.

Amit and Samara were waiting on the sands. I could see Samara waving excitedly. I got out of the water and they both engulfed me in a warm hug.

"I knew you would do it," Amit exclaimed excitedly. "How many yards did you swim?"

"I think around 400 yards back and forth," I panted.

"Awesome," he said.

After a while Penni came up and hugged me too. "You did great," she said.

I smiled. "Thank you," I said gratefully. "Without you I don't think I would have had it in me to get into the water again."

"It was all your efforts, don't thank me for it."

It felt as though a huge burden had been lifted off my shoulders. I was excited as well as thrilled as I finally achieved what I thought would be impossible. I began to head towards the changing rooms which were located near the series of steps. Penni instructed us to change before assembling again near Tower 1 for a brief discussion.

After 15-20 minutes, all of us had assembled near Tower 1. It was almost 10:30 am and the sun was up. The misty shades of grey had been replaced with contours of blue. The water sparkled in the sunlight, reflecting the azure blue sky. By now families began to stream in. Some had placed their vibrant beach towels on the sand. Some of them were already indulging in a game of volleyball. I could spot few surfers on the waves. What a remarkable transformation, I thought. It was just like the vision that was etched in my mind, similar to those pictures that I had seen online.

"So," Penni began, "How many of you have signed up for the Tri Santa Cruz event next week?" A few of them raised their hands.

"Now we all will head towards Depot Park which is about 0.3 miles from here. I hope all of you have brought your bikes. We will practice few transition skills. Any questions about the swim, please feel free to approach me."

Some of them headed back to their vehicles to get the bikes. My family and I waited there to have a talk with Penni.

"Have you signed up for the triathlon event?" she asked.

"Hmm no... still debating whether I should."

"You did good today for a first timer. How is your biking and running?"

"My biking is just fine, though lots of scope for improvement. But I have been running half marathons since 2012."

"Nice. In that case I would recommend that you start off with the Sprint distance. It is just 0.45 miles swim, 12.5 miles biking and 3.1 miles running. You should be fine. Besides there are no cut-offs for the swim."

"Come on Swe, go for it," Amit encouraged me.

I hesitated.

"Where do I buy a wetsuit? And what about the other stuff that I need, like ear plugs and body glide?"

"I would go to any Sports Basement Store. It is worth investing in one if you are planning to pursue this sport. You will get all the stuff you need over there," said Penni.

I thought for a minute. Should I? Should I not? Heck. Why was I thinking so much? This was my dream, right? I took a deep breath and asked another question.

"Are there any cut-offs for completing this Sprint distance triathlon?"

"Oh no, we don't have any cut-offs as such."

"Alright. I will attempt a Sprint distance and see how it goes."

"You are going to be fine," Penni patted me on the shoulder. "Have you got your bike with you?"

"It is in the vehicle."

"Great. Come on up to Depot Park. You will learn some transition skills. I will answer all the queries about the event there."

"So how do we sign up for the event?" asked Amit.

"You could either go online or sign up right here and pay the amount. I have some forms with me in my bag."

"We will do that."

Taking out his wallet, Amit paid the amount to Penni

who was in charge of the event while I filled the form with my details.

"Great," smiled Penni. "You will receive a confirmation mail in a short while. I will see you at Depot Park."

We went to Jake to return his wetsuit.

"Oh hey! How did it go?"

"Not so great in the beginning but managed to finally swim a few laps later on. I just signed up for my first triathlon event."

"Good for you," he beamed.

"Yeah. Hope it goes well."

"I am sure it will."

As we headed up to Depot Park, my heart was thumping with excitement and nervousness. I had mixed feelings, elated that I had signed up for my first triathlon and nervous about how it will go. I braced myself to learn the transition skills after collecting my bike from the car. By now I had begun to enjoy my bike rides. The sheer joy of breezing through the highway gave me a sense of freedom. Unlike in India, there were separate lanes for bikes which made me feel safe. Back in India, I was always anxious about being run over by a bus or a truck. Bikers were treated as specimens that these 'superior' vehicles could run over. It was a pleasant feeling to find respect shown towards bikers by the drivers in the US.

Meanwhile, rest of the participants had gathered at Depot Park. However, I didn't see the folks from

Team Asha. Penni went on to explain on how to set up transition.

"You have to rack your bike like this," she said, as she racked hers on the stand.

I watched closely. The seat of the bike was hung over the rack in a way that the rear wheel was up and the handlebars faced downwards. I practiced racking mine.

She began to talk about how and where to place our things during an event. She spread out a towel on the spot which was below the rear wheel of the bike. She started putting the items needed in the order of the swim, bike and run.

"First place your swim cap, goggles, ear plugs and body glide along with your wetsuit. For the bike, you need your helmet as there will be no riding without a helmet," she stated in her no-nonsense tone. "Besides that, you'll need your biking glasses, gloves, cleats. Most importantly you'll need a toolkit comprising of CO_2 cartridges, a lever and a spare tube. Just in case you get a flat tyre."

I processed all this information. The thought about a flat tyre never crossed my mind until then. I prayed and hoped that it would never happen. We then went on to practice transitioning. I lifted my bike and rode a bit around the parking lot. Then I dismounted, racked the bike and went for a run around the block.

"Good job you guys," Penni cheered.

I really liked the way she encouraged all the newcomers.

She went on to explain about when to get to transition on the race day. The transition would be at Depot Park. "I'd get there at least 90 minutes before the event starts. I recommend you guys do the same. That will get you enough time to set up your things and head to the beach for a warm up swim."

After we wound up, I thanked her and she wished me luck.

I was in high spirits when we sat down at Ideal Bar & Grill for lunch. It was a beautiful eat out joint in Santa Cruz that overlooked the pier. Coupled with nervousness and excitement, I could barely eat my grilled vegetables. I marvelled at how in just a day I had managed to learn a lot about the sport called Triathlon. I knew this was just the beginning.

Just then I spotted Coach Char and called out to him.

He turned in surprise.

"Thank you so much for helping me out there," I muttered gratefully.

"Oh no worries," he smiled.

I asked him about joining Team Asha and he said that the season was coming to an end. He asked me to look it up online. I nodded and continued eating my lunch.

Meanwhile there were folks out there surfing and riding the waves. I watched them in admiration, eager to befriend the ocean. I visualized crossing the finish line and posing with my triathlon medal. What an accomplishment that would be. My first triathlon in a foreign country. I had a week to get ready and decided to speak to Viv when I got back home.

The same evening, I called Viv. It was Sunday morning in India. I told him about signing up for the first Sprint triathlon. He was very happy and encouraging.

"You have been swimming, biking and running regularly. Sprint distance shouldn't be a problem for you. I will send you a plan for this week so that you finish your Sprint distance in a strong manner. I will give you a proper triathlon training plan after you finish this Sprint distance. You can train for an Olympic distance triathlon after that."

I thanked him and excitedly looked forward to the week ahead. I had to visit the Sports Basement Store and also get a formalized plan for the triathlon from Viv.

Chapter 5

Getting into the Tri Mode

"This one step – choosing a goal and sticking to it – changes everything."

– Scott Reed

I had just one week to go for my first triathlon. I headed to the Sports Basement Store as Penni had instructed. It was located in a place called Sunnyvale which was about twenty minutes away from Stanford Campus. I went over to the swim section and gaped in awe at the wide range of wetsuits. I was then approached by one of the staff members who kindly laid out a few wetsuits. I told her about my swim at Santa Cruz and how I had signed up for my first triathlon.

"Oh, good for you," she beamed. "The water in Santa Cruz is cold. You need a thicker wetsuit."

She handed me a pink and grey wetsuit of Zoot brand. I tried it on and the wetsuit turned out to be a perfect fit.

I then bought few ear plugs and a body glide which was also available in the swim section. Along with it, I got a bottle of wetsuit cleaner. It was to be used to hand wash the wetsuit post swim. I also got a tri-suit. This was a one-piece garment that could be worn through the swim, bike and run. I then headed over to the bike section where I procured a safety kit tool with spare tubes for my bike. I recollected Penni having mentioned this at the clinic. I also picked up a box of banana-strawberry Gu gels. Triathlon was an expensive sport in comparison to running.

Once back home and settled, I glanced at the plan that Viv had sent over WhatsApp.

Monday: 0.62 mile swim.

Tuesday: A speed run workout, where I had to run as fast as I could for one minute and run slow the next minute. I had to repeat these eight times.

Wednesday: 15 mile bike ride.

Thursday: 0.5 mile swim and a 4 mile run.

Friday: A recovery ride for 20 minutes.

Saturday: Rest day.

Sunday: Race day.

The week began on a positive note as I began my routine. After dropping Samara at her school cum day care, I biked to the Stanford pool. It was a bright and sunny morning which made it an ideal weather for a swim. Since I had been regularly swimming 0.95 miles in the pool earlier, 0.62 miles felt easy. I noticed that I swam a little faster than usual that particular day. I guess it was due to the excitement of training for an actual race. It made me a lot more charged up. Or perhaps it was the effect of the peanut butter sandwich that I had as my pre-workout meal.

After my swim, I headed home to fix my lunch which was a bowl of lentils and green vegetables. It was usually broccoli, beans or cabbage. My body was used to not consuming rice or Indian bread for many years. And I had run many half marathons in the past. Late afternoon, I would have a cup of green tea accompanied with a fistful of walnuts or a fruit. It was mostly an apple or a bowl of strawberries. Dinner was the same as lunch. On rare occasions whenever I felt hungry, I would snack on Greek unflavoured yogurt.

This was the diet that I followed throughout that week and many weeks after that. The rest of the week followed a similar regime as I diligently followed Viv's plan. Tuesday was spent in the gym where I pushed myself for the run intervals until I was exhausted. Since I had to commute to the pool and the gym by bike, a little bit of biking on a daily basis became a part of this training plan.

My 15 mile bike ride on Wednesday was also a strong one. From my campus accommodation, I biked on Stanford Avenue which led to the Foothill Expressway. I would take a left and keep going on the highway which had a separate section for bikers. To my right, I spotted Stanford

Dish which was a popular trail or hiking and running. I had run there a couple of times. It was a 3.5 mile loop and extremely hilly. The course had gentle rolling hills. I had always enjoyed my rides on this route. Sometimes I would watch other bikers zoom past me and they would flash a smile. It was a smile that I would often exchange with other runners on the road. A smile that was a token of acknowledgement, appreciation and respect for a fellow sportsperson, be it a runner or a biker.

Biking liberated me. With the sun shining on my face and the wind in my hair, I had never felt closer to nature. The cars here always respected bikers, unlike in India where biking often invited danger and death upon oneself. With no separate lanes, bikers had a tough time trying to find space on the roads amidst cars, buses and other two wheelers.

On Thursday, I swam 0.5 miles in the morning. In the evening, around 5:00 pm, I ran 4 miles around the Stanford Campus. Things were going smoothly according to the plan. As the race day edged closer, I felt a queer mix of nervousness and excitement.

After the 20-minute recovery ride, I took my bike to the Bike Connections store. I had one of the technicians check the brakes, fill air and do a check-up to ensure that the bike was fine. In other words, it was called a tune up. Since I had bought it from the same store, they had a complimentary tune up for a year.

I was asked to collect my bike in the evening. I spent Friday afternoon packing as we were to drive to Santa Cruz on Saturday morning. I made a list and quickly checked off the items one by one. This included my wetsuit, tri-suit, a T-shirt, towel, ear plugs, body glide, swim goggles, bike helmet, gloves, bike glasses, a bottle of water that was to be kept on my bike, shoes that would be used both for running as well as on the bike, Garmin watch and a box of Gu gels. I ensured that I took my peanut butter along. Later in the evening, I collected my bike and did a couple of rounds to ensure that it was fine.

On Saturday morning, we drove to Santa Cruz, collected my participation packet which contained by bib number and swim cap. Later we had lunch at one of the restaurants at the pier and watched the sea lions in action. It had been a smooth ride so far.

Little did I realize that my first Sprint distance triathlon will be an eventful one and one hell of a roller coaster ride....

Chapter 6

'Tri'ing to Sprint

*"The miracle isn't that I finished. The miracle is that
I had the courage to start."*

– John Bingham

I almost did not do my first Sprint distance triathlon.

I woke up with butterflies in my stomach. We had stayed over at the Sea & Sand Inn at Santa Cruz, the previous night. It was quite foggy on Race Day morning. It resonated with my mind which was clouded with several questions. Would I survive the swim? Would I have a safe ride without getting a flat tyre? Would I make it to the finish line?

I went through the distance in my mind. It was 0.45 miles swimming, 12.5 miles biking and 3.1 miles running. There were no cut-offs as such I reminded myself. Still I didn't want anything to go wrong. I nibbled a peanut butter sandwich and left it halfway, unable to eat anymore.

"Swe, it's your first triathlon. You are going to need all the energy. Please finish your sandwich," Amit pleaded.

"I can't eat anymore," I muttered. For some reason, the peanut butter tasted like rubber in my mouth and I couldn't get myself to swallow. I choked and reached out for water.

Taking a few deep breaths, I began to get ready. Samara was sleeping peacefully. I looked at her, half wishing I could curl up next to her and go back to sleep. Only to be later reminded that I was here to achieve my goal. A goal that would help me channelize the bouts of loneliness I had begun to face in the Bay area. Maybe triathlon as a sport would help me gain some confidence just like how running did, back in 2012, when I had hit a low phase in my life. I recollected that torrid phase in my life. I had just come out of the hospital after being diagnosed with Ulcerative Colitis. I had lost a lot of blood, strength and my self-confidence. I had to alter my diet and lifestyle which involved a lot of late nights. Life looked bleak and running helped me gain a purpose in life.

At this moment, I never wanted anything so badly in my life. I wanted to finish this Sprint distance at any cost. I put on my blue and black coloured tri-suit and a jacket. I slipped on my Garmin watch. It had a triathlon mode and could be used during swims. Though it was August, early mornings at Santa Cruz were really cold. A chill wave of air greeted me as I opened the door. I was glad that I had my jacket on. I bumped into another participant outside the hotel room. He looked strong and athletic. The surety in the manner he was wheeling his bike made him look like a pro.

"Are you here for the Tri Santa Cruz event?" I asked him.

"I sure am," he grinned.

"Which is the way to Depot Park?"

"Follow me. I'll show you," he said mounting his bike.

I did the same albeit not so gracefully.

Depot Park was just five minutes away and bustling with athletes. They looked a confident lot, sure of what they were doing. On the other hand, I seemed to fumble and my hands began to shake a little. The bike racks were assigned according to bib numbers. I soon found my spot which read 296 – my bib number. The emotions that I encountered now were similar to the feelings during my first day at school. Of feeling lost and not knowing what to do. I looked around to observe other athletes. I racked my bike and began to set up my things. I recollected Penni's instructions from the clinic the previous week where she had mentioned an important point on setting up things in the order of swim, bike and run.

So, I placed my wetsuit, fluorescent colour cap, goggles, ear plugs, body glide, helmet, glasses, fuel belt, running shoes and T-shirt. I placed a sticker with my bib number on the bike stem and on my helmet. I noticed that other athletes had separate bike shoes which I later learnt were called cleats. I remember Penni mentioning them. Being a novice, I was planning on biking with my running shoes.

Volunteers hustled about body marking every athlete. This was a norm followed in every triathlon where all the participants had their bib number marked with a black sketch pen on their left arm and their age on their left calf. I got body marked by a cheerful volunteer who wished me luck.

"Thanks! I am going to need lots of it," I muttered.

I still had an hour to go before my event. I began to apply body glide on my arms and legs as displayed by Penni last week. This would help in slipping on the wetsuit. I slipped on mine. A couple of participants darted admiring looks in my direction.

"That's a nice wetsuit," they remarked.

I smiled basking in the glory of their praise and began to feel better until I walked down to the beach, barefoot.

The sight of the cold and grey ocean was enough to set those nervous bouts again. Just thinking about the experience, the previous week made me feel squeamish. Penni had instructed all of us to do a warm up swim before the event. I looked around to see the beach, it was swarming with participants. It was a flurry of green, pink and fluorescent caps which added colour to the insipid beach.

Some of them had already begun to enter the waves

and swim a few laps. I tiptoed nervously and let the waves brush against my legs. It felt as if a sheet of ice had landed on my feet. I shivered and had half a mind to turn back and return to the cosy warm bed of my hotel room. Just then, all those unpleasant moments at Stanford flashed in my mind. It was a reminder as to why I was here – in search of a new identity and self-confidence.

Taking a deep breath, I waded through the waves until the water reached my hip. I noticed a few other athletes by my side and was comforted by their presence.

"Isn't the water cold?" one of them remarked. I nodded in agreement. The temperature of the water was about 60 degree Fahrenheit.

My teeth started chattering as the water came up to my neck. Closing my eyes, I began to swim using breast strokes as a warm up. After swimming a few laps, I felt slightly better. I noticed how other athletes put their heads down. I still couldn't get myself to put my head inside the ocean water like I did in the swimming pool. The thought of not being able to see anything terrified me, besides the feel of cold water on my face. When I swam to the shore, I enjoyed the feel of the waves pushing me. I got out and glanced at my watch. It was 8:00 am, still half an hour to go before my event commenced.

I stood there watching the Olympic distance participants' line up. Their wave started 30 minutes earlier than mine as their distance was longer. They had to swim 0.95 miles, bike 25 miles and run 6.2 miles. I watched them enter the waters like pros as they swam deftly amidst the waves. How I longed to do that distance someday.

It was soon time for my wave. I stood in line with rest of the participants. Spotting some familiar faces from the swim clinic the previous week, I began to chat with them. It was the first triathlon for some of them which made me feel better. I was not the only one after all. All the athletes had to cross the official timing mat before they entered the waters. There was a small machine attached to the timing mat which beeped every time a participant crossed the mat. However, when I crossed the mat, the machine failed to beep. I was immediately asked to step aside by the race officials.

"Mam, where is your timing chip?" they asked.

My heart suddenly stopped and I felt a surge of panic rising through my veins.

"Timing chip? What timing chip," I wondered frantically.

"The timing chip to be worn on your left ankle."

I looked at the rest of the participants. For the first time, I noticed that they had this thick black strap firmly clasped to their left ankles.

How did they get it? From where? I had no clue. My eyes filled with tears as I looked at the race officials helplessly.

"I have no clue. I don't know. How... oh please. This is my first tri... I have come all the way from India...," breaking into sobs.

They softened down. "Relax mam. You see that guy over there wearing a white cap. He is the race director. He will tell you what to do."

I hurriedly walked up to him with tears streaming down my cheeks.

A man wearing the race director's cap looked at me curiously. It must have appeared strange for him to see a participant in tears just before the swim start. I could almost feel the salt from my tears as they streamed down my cheeks. I barely got the words out of my mouth as I stood in front of him. The other volunteers looked on, all perplexed wondering what happened.

"P... please sir, are you... are you the race director?" I stammered.

He nodded. "What's going on?" he asked kindly.

He had a fair complexion with compassionate brown eyes. I relaxed a bit seeing that he didn't look as stern as I envisioned a race director to be.

"I... I don't seem to have my timing chip... I mean I didn't know there was one."

He looked puzzled.

"Didn't you get it at the packet pickup yesterday? It should have been there along with your bib number and swim cap."

"I... I don't know sir... I know my cap was there and so was my bib number for my bike, helmet and the run... but...."

"Are you staying here?"

"Yes."

"Is there anyone I can call?"

"Yes, my husband... His number is...."

For some reason, my mind went blank. I simply couldn't recollect his number. It had just been a month since I got here. I had stored his number on my mobile but not in my memory. I looked at the race director with terror in my eyes. Oh dear, what must he be thinking, I thought.

Just then I spotted Amit and Samara walking towards me. He seemed concerned with a questionable expression on his face.

"What happened Swe?" he asked hurrying towards me.

"My timing chip... It is missing." Turning to the race director, I said, "That's my husband."

He hurriedly took down Amit's number and asked where we were staying. Amit offered to look for the timing chip in the hotel.

Meanwhile the race had already begun. I watched the elites get into the water. They swam deftly amidst the waves looking like mermen. I felt a wave of panic seize me as I turned to the race director uncertainly.

"My race...," I mumbled looking pleadingly into his face.

"Oh yes. You can go ahead. Wait let me note down your bib number."

I looked at him in disbelief and a glimmer of hope.

"Really?"

"Yes, just go ahead. If we find your timing chip, you can wear it. Else we will just give you your overall time. You may not get your chip timing."

At that moment, I felt such a surge of gratitude that the word 'thank you' seemed so miniscule. Yet I couldn't think of anything else to say.

"Oh! Thank you! You don't know how much this means to me," I almost tripped over my words.

I watched him saying something into his microphone as he gestured me to join the other participants in my wave.

The volunteers didn't say anything this time but let me pass the timing mat. I was still shaken from what happened and wiped my tears.

"Hey, don't sweat it. It happens sometimes. You will just not get your split timings," one of the fellow participants reassured me kindly.

I looked at her gratefully while her blue eyes exuded concern. It was for the second time that day when I felt the word 'thank you' would sound inconsequential.

The horn blew and it was race time. All the participants rushed to the water and got in smoothly while I took my time. I switched on my watch, entered the waters cautiously and began swimming breast strokes. Since it was the first stroke that I learnt in swimming as a little girl, I'd instinctively use it every time I was in the water before I switched to freestyle. This was precisely what I did today.

Wading through the waves, my heart was already pounding fast due to the unforeseen palpable tension before the race. I was suddenly feeling exhausted from all the crying, ashamed of myself for behaving like a school kid. However, I couldn't help it, considering how close I came to missing out on my dream of doing a triathlon. I swam a few yards doing breast strokes before I switched to free style. The other participants were way ahead of me. Obviously, they had a lot more experience and were putting their faces inside the water. A streamlined position helps a person glide faster in water. It was my first time I reminded myself every time I'd see my fellow participants going faster and further. I kept my head up and began to do freestyle. This way I could keep sight of the big orange buoys which were placed as markers in the water. I was almost out of breath when I reached the first buoy. I held on to it while the volunteers stationed on the kayaks looked at me with concern.

"Are you alright?" they asked.

I nodded panting.

After a few minutes, I began to swim again. 0.45 miles in the ocean suddenly felt like a huge distance and it seemed to go on forever. When on land, I could run this distance in about 4-5 minutes. The waves were a powerful force I thought, as they kept hitting my face. In the meantime, participants from the wave after us began to overtake me. I froze in panic which made me lose my breath. My stomach was in knots and I was panting as though I had just run up a really steep hill. The cold water was extracting all my energy as well. Focusing back on my strokes, I soon reached the second buoy where a volunteer on a kayak cheered for me.

"You are almost there. Just keep going. You got this one," he said.

He had a perfectly round face and a smile that reminded me of Charlie Brown – one of the characters from the *Peanuts* cartoon.

I began to swim towards the shore which appeared quite close. Swimming in an ocean can make things seem deceptive especially with regards to distance. You feel that you are almost there but then realize that you still have a long way to go. It felt like forever but I managed to reach the shore in one piece. Panting, I scrambled on my feet and ran towards the timing mat. I spotted Amit and Samara waiting for me. He was clicking my photo as I walked towards him. Running on sand seemed next to impossible after a swim in the freezing ocean.

"Did you find my timing chip?" I asked him.

"No. It doesn't seem to be anywhere. You keep going. The race director said he's got it sorted out."

I felt as though a huge burden had been lifted off my shoulders. For the first time that morning, I felt relaxed.

I began to unzip my wetsuit. The hardest part was getting out of the wetsuit that clung to you like second skin. I ripped one sleeve off and then the other until it hung till my waist. Okay that wasn't so bad. When I tried to pull off the wetsuit from both my legs, I struggled. I sat down on the sands and after a bit of an effort, managed to yank it off completely. Phew! What a relief I thought as I handed my dripping and muddy wetsuit to my husband. Usually handing over wetsuits to family/friends wasn't allowed in other races apparently, but Penni mentioned the previous week that she'd make it an exception in this particular event. I glanced at my watch. I had taken about 25 minutes.

Transition 1: With the wetsuit off, I felt as though I could fly. I ran towards the ramp in my dripping blue and black tri-suit while the onlookers and volunteers cheered for me. Quite a few participants had placed their flip flops next to the ramp and slipped them on before they ran to Depot Park. I continued running barefoot, crossing the railway tracks and making my way towards the transition. A few other athletes were huffing and puffing. Some paused to catch their breath while I continued running. My lungs felt as though they were on fire and I was breathless by the time I reached my bike.

I plonked down and took a bite of my Gu gel. The banana-strawberry flavour melted in my mouth inducing about 100 calories straightaway into my system. I took off my cap and goggles and shoved them into the bag. I slipped on my running T-shirt as I was shivering in my tri-suit. It was supposedly summer time being the month of August but Santa Cruz seemed to think otherwise. It was quite cold. I buckled my helmet, put on my gloves and shoes and wheeled my bike towards the area from where participants could mount their bikes.

I reached the area which said, 'Mount bike'. Just as I crossed the timing mat, a volunteer pointed out asking, "I don't see your timing chip."

I froze…

My head felt hot and my heart almost stopped for a minute, wondering if I was going to be asked to discontinue the race. Taking a deep breath, I looked at the volunteer with a nervous expression on my face.

"Um, the race director said I could do the race and he has got it sorted out. You can ask him. This is my bib number," I mumbled pointing to the rectangular sheet pinned on my T-shirt that read 296.

The volunteer looked confused for a minute, but then he let me go on my bike ride after noting down my bib number.

Riding those wheels – A steep uphill greeted me just outside Depot Park. My lungs burned as I pedalled up the slope. The volunteers standing there cheered and said, "Just this one hill. After that it's all a flat route." Huffing my way up, I turned right on to West Cliff Drive and began to enjoy the views of the ocean. The bike route was two rounds of the 6.2 mile loop and was closed for traffic. It was a treat to enjoy the roads to myself without worrying about a car behind me.

As I pedalled along the roads in Santa Cruz, I occasionally kept hearing "on your left" by other bikers. This meant that you had to give way to others to overtake you. I happily let them pass, not letting the competitive feeling creep in. This was my first triathlon and besides I strongly believed that the only competition was with oneself. I let my shoulders relax and posed for the photographers. Another set of volunteers kept ringing small bells, cheering all the participants. Amidst this bike ride, I chanted a mantra that I usually do whenever I'd want anything to go smooth. *Om Gan Ganpathaye Namaha* (salutations to the elephant faced God). During my childhood, I had heard the story of Lord Ganesha's birth and how praying to him would help in removing any obstacles. It remained etched in my mind ever since.

All of a sudden it then struck me that I was actually in a triathlon event. Goosebumps filled my arms and it wasn't just because of the cold weather. A shiver ran down my spine and my heart was thumping loudly. I almost forgot about the incident that occurred that morning. I breezed downhill up to Depot Park and got down from my bike. I had taken about 52 minutes.

Transition 2: I wheeled my bike into my spot and racked it. I breathed a sigh of relief for not getting a flat tyre. Just one more hurdle to go. It took me hardly a minute to grab my Gatorade bottle and set out for the run.

Embracing the strides – I dashed out of transition and upped my speed. "Good running. Going strong," shouted a volunteer. I waved and soon found myself on West Cliff Drive. Running after biking is tough on the legs as they end up feeling wobbly. Going up that slope again caused my breathing to become rapid. Surviving the slope, I began to find my rhythm. Having done several half marathons and one full marathon, running wasn't that tough. The runner in me eventually found my comfortable pace. I could hear the sound of waves and the sun was beginning to come out, painting a rather pretty picture of Cowell Beach.

At the turn around point, I increased my pace further. I couldn't wait to embrace the finish line and get my first triathlon medal. It was too good to be true. It was all downhill from there as I turned from West Cliff Drive into Depot Park. I could hear the emcee's voice calling out the participant's name as they crossed the finish line. With every step, I seemed to be inching closer to the finish line. I was just 300 yards from my dream. It was surreal. I felt a pulsating rush through my veins and my heart was pounding loudly. As I edged closer, I saw the arch to the finish line. I had seen plenty of these arches during several running events that I had participated in. However, this one was different. It was the finish line of my very first triathlon event. A wave of triumph hit me as I crossed the finish line with the emcee calling out, "Swetha Amit from Stanford."

A kind volunteer garlanded the medal. I gazed at it in delight. It was a beautiful red coloured one with palm trees carved on it. It had 2017 Tri Santa Cruz written on it. I felt like a kid with a Christmas present.

Another participant had just crossed the finish line after me. I watched the volunteer remove the timing chip from a participant's ankle. Just as they were about to ask me for my timing chip, I spotted the race director and Penni, standing along with Amit and Samara. The race director gestured to the volunteer. He had noted my time. It was 1:53:39.

"All good?" he asked.

"Oh. Thank you so much. You don't know how much this means to me," I said breathlessly.

His eyes twinkled and he smiled, "Congratulations."

I hugged and thanked Penni. "Be careful next time about your timing chip," she said.

"I will," I replied wondering how and where that black strap could disappear from my packet.

I collected my bike and put the rest of my belongings into a big bag. Handing the bag to Amit, I lifted my bike and posed with my medal. My spirits were high and my heart soared. I felt like doing a victory dance around Depot Park.

"So how was the experience?" Amit asked later when we were in our room, getting ready to leave. We were packing our stuff and loading them into the car.

"It was wonderful. I mean I was stressed initially especially about that timing chip. But after the race director reassured me, it was great. This sport is something Amit. It gave me that surge of adrenalin rush – something that I haven't felt in a long time. I definitely want to do more triathlons."

"I am sure you will. We are going to be here till next July."

As I lifted my travel bag, my eyes fell on an object near the bed. I walked towards it, half fearing that it might be an insect or a reptile. All I saw was a long piece of black strap similar to what I'd seen the participants wearing on their left ankle that morning. The timing chip had somehow fallen out of the packet. I picked it up and looked at it in disbelief. If it were a human, I'd have reprimanded it by now as its absence almost cost me my dream. Deep down, I made a mental note to be more careful next time I do a triathlon event. The timing chip would be the first thing that I'd strap around my left ankle. I strongly believed that every sporting event taught you something. This was my first lesson from my first triathlon event.

Chapter 7

Toying with A New Sport

*"The future belongs to those who believe in
the beauty of their dreams."*

– Eleanor Roosevelt

I was still reeling over my first ever triathlon event. When I came back home later, I called Viv and told him about my experience and my zest to keep training for it.

"Well I'll put you on a plan for an Olympic distance. That's 0.95 miles swimming, 25 miles biking and 6.2 miles running."

"I don't think I am ready for an Olympic distance," I practically yelped. I couldn't imagine swimming 0.95 miles in the ocean. I definitely needed more practice in the ocean. I made a mental note to mail Penni and ask her about open water swim sessions. Since these swim clinics were only for a day, it would help if I could get into a regular training mode in open waters.

"I think you are ready for an Olympic. Keep training and we'll see how it goes," said Viv.

In the meanwhile, I mailed Penni and asked her about the open water sessions. She replied saying that there was a group called Westend Wharf & Wine Swim Club which usually swims on Friday evenings and Sunday mornings at Cowell Beach in Santa Cruz. I looked them up on Facebook and joined the group. However, I couldn't make it to the swim sessions due to certain time constraints. Friday evening was a little difficult with both Amit's classes and Samara's school. And it didn't seem fair to wake up Amit and Samara early every Sunday morning. I decided to join a swim clinic if it was scheduled on Saturdays.

Viv sent me the training plan for the Olympic distance triathlon. He said that since it was on my bucket list, this plan would make me stronger. When I went through it, I saw that there were two workouts on most days.

Mondays were rest days.

Tuesdays included running speed intervals. This was a one minute fast run followed by another slow run. The repetitions were between ten to fifteen sets. In the evening, there were bike intervals. This included a warm up for twenty minutes. Two minutes of fast spinning with one minute of slow recovery. This was repeated five times and then the cool down was for another fifteen minutes.

Wednesdays were for swims. The distance varied

between 1-1.2 miles. Sometimes in the evenings, there would be an hour of biking or strength training.

Thursdays included brick training. Brick training is a session in which you do two disciplines back to back. This involved a bike ride followed by a run. Sometimes it would include a swim followed by a bike ride. In my case it was mostly a bike ride followed by a run. The duration was a 60 minutes bike ride followed by twenty minutes of running. It was really hard to run after biking. The legs felt like bricks which is how perhaps the name brick training was coined.

Fridays included another swim. The distance was usually a mile. I would do strength training again in the evening.

Saturdays were reserved for the longer bike rides, which was usually a 26-30 mile ride.

Sundays were allotted for long runs, between 8-10 miles. Being a half marathoner, I would sometimes end up running 12 miles.

My routine continued as before. Dropping Samara at her school and then heading to finish my first workout of the day. I would come back and fix lunch which was usually vegetables and lentils. In the afternoons whenever I felt hungry, I would snack on an apple or fix myself another peanut butter sandwich. I also included some egg whites, grilled Salmon and Quinoa in my diet since this particular training regime was a little more intense.

Three weeks had already flown by and I could still feel the endorphins from the finish line of the Tri Santa Cruz event. The prospect of doing three different sports in one event certainly caught my fancy. Like a kid who had stumbled upon a new toy, I couldn't get enough of this sport called the triathlon. I wanted more such events under my kitty. For some reason, running seemed pale in comparison. Probably, because I had been running for five years now. There was a part of me that wanted to prove that my first triathlon hadn't been a fluke. I felt that I had it in me to do more such events.

Being the end of summer, my writing classes for the term were over. My next course would commence by September end. I had an entire month ahead of me. It was a Friday evening and I had finished my workouts for the day. I had to pickup Samara from the day care by 6:00 pm. I glanced at the clock. I still had an hour. Quickly grabbing my laptop, I began to surf the net for triathlon events. After minutes of searching, I stumbled upon an event called the Mermaid Series. The name sounded familiar. Oh yes! It was at the Tri Santa Cruz clinic. I remembered Penni asking this lady, "So you are doing the Olympic at the Mermaid Series, right?" The lady nodded and someone remarked that they had done the Mermaid event last year.

It must be a well-organized event, I thought. I scanned the website for further details. Usually most triathlon events had a swim clinic organized just for a day. This was for those who were new to open water swims. The swim clinic was scheduled for September 16th at Capitola Beach which was close to Santa Cruz. I checked the main event date which was October 7th. I immediately signed up for the Sprint distance which involved 0.45 miles swimming, 12.5 miles biking and 3.1 miles running. I didn't yet muster the courage to venture into the Olympic distance which was double the distance. Participants were required to bring similar items as listed in the Tri Santa Cruz clinic. Only this time, I didn't have to take my bike along.

Capitola Beach was roughly an hour away from Stanford. Accompanied by Amit and Samara, I set off for yet another swim in the ocean. Samara had brought her small bucket and spade in hopes of building a sand castle. I was in the meanwhile building my dreams about becoming a serious triathlete. I was restless and impatient to get ahead in this journey.

It was a bright sunny morning. The waves appeared calm and blue while the sands sparkled in the sunlight. Few participants had already assembled near the swim clinic. I recognized one lady from the Tri Santa Cruz clinic and smiled at her. The Mermaid Series event was an all-women's event so barring the race director, all those assembled on the beach were ladies. A quick round of introductions was done. The nuances of open water swim were explained. It was similar to what I had learnt at the Tri Santa Cruz clinic. We were told that we'd be swimming the Sprint distance.

For some reason, I was calm that morning. My stomach didn't twist itself into knots like it did at Cowell Beach. Was it because I had one Sprint distance to my credit? Or maybe just looking at the calm blue ocean ahead of me soothed my nerves. I watched the gentle waves brush against the shore. The ocean seemed to exude a certain warmth and friendliness.

"Beautiful day, isn't it?" a voice interrupted my thoughts.

I looked up to see that it was the race director. I agreed wholeheartedly, "Oh yes it looks beautiful."

After a few minutes, I began to put on my wetsuit. My first swim clinic with Penni helped me slip on the wetsuit with a lot more confidence. I walked towards the water and let the waves brush against my legs. It was definitely warmer than Cowell Beach. I watched others warm up and noticed how they first let in some water inside their wetsuit before they fully dived in. I did the same. After about 10 minutes of warm up, we were all set to go. Accompanied by a few volunteers on the kayak and some who were swimming with the group, I was geared to go.

This time again, I couldn't get myself to put my face inside the water. I tried once only to choke and splutter so I continued swimming with my head up. A volunteer swimming next to me suggested that it would be a good idea to put my head down. I nodded but still couldn't get myself to do so. Mine was probably the weirdest freestyle anyone would have seen. Nevertheless, I continued swimming. Couple of times I felt a little intimidated by the waves but the volunteers around egged me on. The presence of the kayak assured me that safety was just within an arm's reach in case anything went wrong.

Before I realized, I had reached the shore. I got out of the water and looked behind to see that there were few more people in the water. I glanced at my Garmin watch and it showed that I had completed my swim in 22 minutes. I felt strong enough to go for another round, if I had company and support.

"Hey Swe, how did it go?" Amit asked as I approached them. Samara and he had managed to build a beautiful sand castle. "You seem to look strong."

I was surprised at myself. Just a couple of months back, I was struggling and today I had a good swim. I shook my head in disbelief. My breathing seemed normal and I wasn't panting like how I did at Cowell Beach.

"Mama look, sand castle!" Samara tittered and pulled me towards her to take a look at her creation.

"It's beautiful," I remarked and her face lit up with joy.

Everything and everyone seemed to radiate happiness that morning.

"So Swe, how did it feel this time?" Amit asked for the second time.

"Oh, sorry! It went great. I mean I don't know how but this time I felt a lot better. Stronger than I had at Cowell Beach."

I walked towards the rest of the participants and began to collect my belongings.

"So how did it go?" the race director asked.

"Pretty good."

"So, you have signed up for the event?"

"Yeah!"

"Great. Are you doing the Olympic?"

I paused as an idea began to form in my head, 'Should I...'

"Swe, I think you should just go for the Olympic distance," Amit came up behind me.

I hesitated. The prospect seemed too tempting. Was I ready to take the plunge? I realized that this was my opportunity otherwise I had to wait until April as the triathlon season was almost over in the Bay area.

I took a deep breath and my heart skipped a beat. My hands began to shake and I felt like an electric shock had passed through my body. Finally, I mustered all my courage and looked at the race director.

"Is there any cut-off time?"

"No cut-offs at all. We want all participants to just finish," he said reassuringly.

"Is it possible for me to upgrade?"

"Yes. Let me put you on to Stephanie." He beckoned

a lady and asked her to note down my details and collect the remaining amount.

Before I realized it, I was signed up for the Olympic distance triathlon. Just as I had envisioned, I was taking the steps towards my dream. I felt this sudden surge of excitement. If all goes well, October 7th, 2017 will be a day that I would treasure forever. I would officially be a triathlete.

Later when I went home to tell Viv – my coach, he was pleased and said, "I think you should go ahead. The plan I was giving you all this while was for the Olympic distance only. So, you will be fine. I will taper it a week before your event."

I continued training hard. Before I knew it, just a week was left before my event. The taper plan included a 45 minute ride on Tuesday, 0.62 mile swim on Wednesday, a 4 mile run on Thursday. Friday was a rest day since my event was on a Saturday.

Everything seemed to be going as per the schedule. Little did I realize that an accident would almost cost me my dream?

Chapter 8

The Fall

"The greatest glory lies not in never falling but rising every time you fall."

– Confucius

WHAM!!!

For a second I didn't know what hit me. Everything appeared like a blur on Foothill Expressway. My head felt a little dizzy. My heart was almost in my mouth and my chest felt tight. I was quite shaken as though someone had rattled all the bones in my body. What had just happened? I mean one minute I was riding my bike smoothly. The next, I was lying on the road. I wasn't sure how I lost balance and slid from my bike.

I blinked my eyes a couple of times. The cars whizzed past me on my left. Thankfully, I had fallen to my right which was on the biking lane and beyond which a pavement with some shrubs. My bike was a few feet away from me. I was just about to get up slowly when I heard a voice.

"Hey, are you okay?"

I turned to see a concerned man who had stopped his car and walked towards me. He was tall and lanky. From his facial features, I could make out that he was of Asian origin.

"I saw you fall off your bike," he said.

I turned to him and pointed towards my bike, "Is my bike okay?" I asked feebly.

He walked over to my fallen bike. My beautiful Felt brand bike had become my regular ally in my adventures in the Bay area including my first triathlon event. It was heart wrenching to see the usually sturdy bike strewn across the road like a dead corpse. He picked it up and examined it carefully, "It seems okay."

I was relieved to hear this. It felt as though a huge weight had been lifted off my shoulders. By now I couldn't imagine my life without a bike. It had been three months since I landed in California. I still didn't have a driver's license. My only other mode of transportation was Uber. Riding a biking gave me a different sort of a thrill. Besides it was the key to fulfil all my triathlon dreams.

I began to examine my hands and feet. I didn't seem to have any bones broken. What I did have was a profusely bleeding right knee. It was cut really deep and looked like a sausage tossed in ketchup. My right arm was scrapped badly as well and it looked like as though someone had grilled it. I could see the pink flesh oozing out. In fact, my wounds looked so bad that the man asked if he should call 911. I shook my head.

"I think I will just finish my ride today and go back home," I said.

He looked at me with uncertainty, probably wondering what kind of a lunatic would go biking with a bleeding knee and arm. But that was me – a little eccentric and mad like how most budding runners and triathletes proclaim themselves to be. Mad enough to not discontinue my workout as it was the last rung of my training schedule before my big day. I had this problem of not wanting to leave things halfway. It created a sort of incomplete feeling.

The Olympic distance triathlon was just a few days away. I wanted to convince myself that it was just a fall and that things were normal.

"Are you sure?" he asked apprehensively.

I nodded.

He shook his head and went back to his car hesitatingly. His brow was furrowed in worry and I could sense that he wasn't happy leaving me in this condition. I mounted on my bike and thanked him profusely with a grin as a reassurance that I was fine. I began to pedal and continued riding my bike.

He drove past me and shouted, "Take care."

I nodded and diverted my attention to the bike. It seemed normal except that the gears were not changing as swiftly as before. Definitely needs a visit to the bike store, I decided. I hoped that they could rectify it before Saturday which was when my event was scheduled. It was Tuesday evening already.

I had been seriously training for the last few weeks. For days, I visualized myself crossing the finish line to officially be declared as a triathlete. I sincerely hoped that this bruise wouldn't come in the way of my dreams.

Thereafter, it was a cautious ride on the highway and I managed to get home in one piece. I ensured that I biked slowly. I did not experience any kind of muscle pull or strain. It was just my knee and arm burning due to the outer layer of my skin scraped. I suppose a little ice would help.

The trees on the highway had begun to change colours depicting the arrival of fall season. What a contrast between my fall and the season. The red shades on the leaves portrayed a pretty sight while my red knee and arm projected an image from a horror flick.

I reached home in one piece and immediately washed my wounds. Despite my attempts to ice them, the bleeding refused to stop. I called up the Palo Alto Medical Foundation Emergency Care. When I explained my situation to the person on the other end, she asked me to come over immediately. Since it was just a few minutes away from home, I hopped on my bike and reached there.

The doctor was a kind faced lady who examined me carefully. She had blond hair and blue eyes with a sharp nose. I had already briefed her about my event.

"That looks bad. Did you actually managed to bike for 40 minutes with that wound?" she asked.

I nodded.

"Well, I must say you are one gutsy girl," she exclaimed. She asked me to raise my arms and stretch my legs. Finally, she seemed convinced that I didn't have any fracture. I winced in pain as she cleaned my wounds. It felt as though 100 needles were piercing through my body.

"I know it hurts," she looked at me sympathetically. "Your event is on Saturday, right?" she said trying to distract me from the pain.

I nodded.

She went on to tell me about her brother who did triathlons as well. I listened intently and was inspired by some of her brother's feats. Apparently, he had done the Ironman distance which involved 2.4 miles swimming, 112 miles biking and 26.2 miles running.

"Well as long as you are feeling fine, go ahead. Just apply this antibiotic cream and change your bandages every day. The wounds should heal in ten days and the scars will disappear over time," she said when she was finally done. "You may want to take some rest for the next three days so that you will be fresh for your triathlon event."

"Sure," I replied.

When I reached home, Amit had already picked up Samara from day care.

"Hey, are you okay?" he asked concerned and did a double take when he saw the thick bandages on my knee and arm. "Goodness! How did this happen? Are you sure you are okay?"

Samara came prancing around me, "Mama! Are you fine?"

I reassured both of them that I was fine. I plonked myself on the sofa, suddenly exhausted. I explained to Amit about what happened. He was really worried and asked me to take rest.

"Are you sure you will be able to do the event? I am feeling so bad Swe. You have been training for months for this."

"I will do this, no matter what. The doctor has given me a go-ahead sign. It is just a physical bruise." I closed my eyes.

Amit and Samara left me to rest on the sofa for a while, knowing that I probably needed some time alone.

I just rested it out for the next few days. I had dropped off my bike at Bike Connections to rectify the gears and another tune up. The staff gave me a sympathetic look at my bandaged arm and knee. They assured me that my bike would be fine by Friday. It was tiring not to work out and sit on the couch the entire day. My body was used to that daily dose of adrenaline rush and endorphins from my workouts which it was deprived of now. But I knew it was for the best. I was restless and kept tracing back to the accident wondering how and why it had occurred. I had biked on Foothill Expressway several times before. Was it just sheer bad luck that I had a fall or was I getting too conceited about my fitness levels and was a victim of the famous saying, 'Pride comes before a fall?'

Suddenly the image of that Asian man's mortified face popped up in my head. I chuckled at the thought of what he must have been feeling when I told him I was going for a ride with that bleeding knee and arm. Feeling slightly better, I opened my laptop and began to check my email. The organizers of the Mermaid Series triathlon event had sent an email. It contained details about the event which included the packet pickup and the agenda of the race day. This time I made a mental note to go through the items at the packet pickup venue and ensure that my timing chip was there.

I browsed through their website again. There were no cut-offs and it clearly stated that they just wanted all the participants to reach the finish line. It was also mentioned that those who finished the Olympic distance would be given the title of a 'Mighty Mermaid' and also a beautiful mermaid shaped medal. Since childhood, I always had a fascination for those mystical creatures. *The Little Mermaid* by Danish author Hans Christian Andersen was my favourite story back then. It was a folklore that mermaids brought bad luck and caused ships to sink. I hoped that this mermaid would bring me luck and help me fulfil my dream of being a triathlete.

I chewed my fingernails and pondered deeply. Would I cross the finish line? What if I fell off my bike during the event? I cursed myself for having been careless. I wished I could turn back in time and change the course of events. I knew it was no use crying over spilt milk, in this case a wounded arm and knee.

When I went to collect my bike, the guy at Bike Connections said it was good to go and asked me to take care of myself. I looked at my bike which was placed in a corner across the hall. Sturdy and strong even after being knocked over. Reminded me of those instances in the boxing ring, where champions get up and fight despite being bruised and knocked over several times. I was reminded of Sylvester Stallone's movie *Rocky Balboa*. From that moment onwards, my bike was christened as 'Rocky'. I wasn't sure if every triathlete named their bike but I was crazy enough to do so.

On Friday night, I tossed and turned in my sleep. I had collected my packet from the pickup place at Title Nine Store at Palo Alto. The nice lady at the counter went over the items with me which included my timing chip, bib which read number 1 and a fluorescent colour cap. I mentally ran over the sequence of the events. I would come out of the swim, pull off my wetsuit, change into my cycling gear and bike the course. I would come back, rack my bike, place my helmet and go for a run. I visualized crossing the finish line and having that beautiful medal garlanded on my neck. A mighty mermaid, I thought and slowly drifted off to sleep....

Chapter 9

A Mighty Mermaid

"Pain is temporary, quitting lasts forever."
– Lance Armstrong

I woke up on Saturday morning with knots in my stomach. My right arm and knee were still sore from the bruises. The antibiotic cream prescribed by the doctor was working well but then it had been only three days since that brutal fall on the highway. I carefully removed the bandage and put another fresh one around it. For a moment, I wondered if the blood-stained bruises would attract the sharks only to remind myself that I'd be in a wetsuit. The coaches at both the swim clinics assured me that our wetsuits were designed to protect us. It would be my armour against my battle with the waves, I thought.

I had already packed my things the day before. This time I double checked to see if the timing chip was there in the packet which I had collected from the packet pickup.

I slipped on my tri-suit and a jacket. My daughter was still sleepy as we put her on the car seat and strapped the seat belt around her. The bike was tucked away at the back of the car.

It was still dark at Capitola. I could see the full moon beaming from the sky as I entered the transition area at 6:30 am. It filled me with feelings of dread as I recollected my memories of the beach on a full moon day. The waves would be even more restless and choppy than usual. It was otherwise slated to be a warm day.

Volunteers were already stationed at the transition area and they directed me to my designated stand. "All mighty mermaids on that side," they told me. Participants of the Olympic distance were called the mighty mermaids at this Mermaid Series triathlon event. I assembled my bike, laid down my mat and placed my running T-shirt, shoes, helmet, bike glasses and few Gu gels. I zipped up my wetsuit firmly and immediately strapped the timing chip around my left ankle. I pressed it a few times till I was sure that it wouldn't fall off. I tucked it inside my wetsuit and prayed that it would stay till the very end. I then slipped on my cap designated for my wave time and held the swim goggles in my hand. That queasy feeling was back again and I remembered feeling the same way before my final exams. My heart fluttered like an anxious bird trying to escape from its cage as I made my way towards the beach. I knew there were no cut-off times for this race. I could go slow and finish the race.

It was a 0.4 mile walk and by the time I reached the start point, most of the participants were already there. Some of them were taking a warm up dip in the ocean. I slowly entered the water and found it unexpectedly warm.

"The sand on the beach is a lot cooler than the water," one of my co-participants joked with me. I smiled faintly. We were all asked to assemble near the start point. I stood there listening to the instructions, my hands shaking slightly. At the countdown of ten, I looked up at the sky and offered a silent prayer. Would I reach the finish line and earn that medal? Would weeks of hard work go down the drain? At the sound of the horn, I ran and entered the ocean, waiting to be engulfed by the waves as I prepared myself to overcome the first hurdle towards the finish line.

Riding the wave – The warm water made me get into a rhythm easily. I used freestyle which was highly recommended for speed. I noticed a couple of women using breast strokes and they seemed to move faster than I did. Now I had been practicing swimming long distances on a regular basis except for the previous week since I had a fall from my bike and was advised complete rest by the doctor until the main event. I watched a couple of women hanging on to the paddle boat to catch their breath. They must have gone too fast, I thought to myself. A mistake that many participants make at the beginning of their run or triathlon. I continued with my strokes taking in the number of paddle boats around me – the volunteers ensured that we were fine.

We were instructed to swim past three orange buoys to our left shoulder. While swimming in the ocean, one was bound to lose direction and visibility if they didn't keep sighting once in a while by putting their heads up. Due to this fear, I kept my head up while swimming and probably this was why my pace had slowed down.

"Try putting your head down," one of the volunteers stationed on a kayak told me.

I was almost close to the shore so I continued going. Others had practically rushed out of the water and I was the only one in the ocean, besides the kind-hearted volunteers of course who kept egging me on.

"Good job," they said as I edged towards the shore which melted all those panic attacks that I had when I noticed that I was the lone participant, literally speaking. I comforted myself saying that the other participants were probably used to swimming in the ocean since their childhood. Coming from India, I never swam in open waters until I reached California in July 2017 at a couple of swim clinics.

I noticed the sun coming out at that time almost as though reassuring me that I wasn't alone. I blinked and looked at it gratefully, for once glad that the sun was out unlike other times where I would remember cursing it for ruining the weather during a long run. It wasn't every day that I would get to enjoy the ocean, I thought and decided to bask in the waves which were a little restless that particular day as I had expected. The choppy waves made me feel giddy and my stomach churned. Those familiar symptoms of nausea were finding their way into my system. Not wanting to succumb to them, I mentally made a note to keep going.

I pretended to be a mermaid as I swam across to the shore. As a little girl, these mystical creatures fascinated me due to their unique appearances and I was always intrigued by life under the ocean and the treasures that were concealed by the superficial waves. Their continuous lashing on the shore and pulling back seemed like a sort of protective stance to fiercely guard these hidden 'treasures'.

I finally reached the shore and glanced at my watch which read 43 minutes. Not bad, I thought as it was much better than my one mile swim in the pool back at the Stanford gym. I met Amit and Samara at the beach, quickly gave them a hug and rushed towards the transition area.

Transition 1: My heart was pounding loudly and my breathing was rapid. I felt as though someone had drained my body out of oxygen. I just wished someone would hand me those oxygen pumps that I often saw the NFL players using as they stood on the sidelines waiting for their turn. Heck! What was I thinking? That was NFL and this was a triathlon. They were pros and I was just a recreational novice. Meanwhile I was trying to get my wetsuit off which was an even more arduous task than completing the actual Olympic triathlon distance. After managing to wriggle off from it amidst all the cheers and claps from the volunteers, I finally put on my T-shirt, helmet, goggles and mounted on my bike. I took about 12 minutes.

Riding amidst the redwoods – My bib number read '1' and I could hear whispers of people around saying, "Hey look she is number 1." A steep hill greeted me at the very beginning of the bike course. It felt like an ugly demon which had raised its head, mocking and challenging me to get past it. I sighed and walked up my bike. I couldn't help thinking that walking upside down on my arms seemed easier than pedaling up that gigantic slope. I reached a point when I knew it looked safe enough to set the wheels rolling. The initial route went past some main roads along with the ongoing traffic. However, the volunteers on the road guided me in a systematic manner and I soon found myself biking away from the chaos and entering the magical woods. An arch of redwood trees stood tall and proud as I huffed and puffed the way up those inclines. There was a point when I had to get off my bike again and walk up.

"Hey, are you okay?" I heard a voice from behind me. It was a lady who had also got off her bike and was walking.

I nodded and mumbled saying how tough a course this was.

"Yes, it's a little hilly," she replied cheerfully. "It's just up to that point after which we can get on our bikes and start pedalling.

"Are you doing the Olympic distance?" I asked her.

"I am actually taking part in the relay where I am doing the cycling and running bit."

Relay was an option at the event where a team of two or three could take part with each person doing one division each or one person could do two divisions like in the case of this lady.

"What about you?" she asked.

"I am doing the individual Olympic," I replied.

"Oh wow, that's amazing. I can never do the swimming bit. I am not a strong swimmer." She looked at me impressed. "Kudos to you."

"Thanks!" I mumbled.

"Hey, you are number one (referring to my bib number) and that should get you through," she smiled.

I smiled back and suddenly felt a sudden spurt in my energy levels. I had read somewhere that a kind word possessed the power to lift one's spirits really high when they hit bouts of low. Today I was actually a recipient to this as I mounted my bike and turned at a point which took us on a long downhill course. Now I was extremely cautious while going downhill as my bike fall happened on a similar terrain on the highway few days earlier. Scarred by that incident, I clutched my brakes lest I go too fast and fall down again. I couldn't bear to hurt myself again, not in the middle of the race when I was so close to my goal. I had dreamt about and waited for this moment for several weeks. Days and hours went into training for this event. I watched others zoom past me including the lady who walked up with me.

"Feels good, now doesn't it?" she waved and I returned her smile mouthing a silent 'thanks' for her helpful gesture a few minutes ago.

The rest of the course was a breeze and the challenge arose when I had to do this loop one more time as per the prescribed distance for the Olympic distance participants. This time, I held my nerve and managed to complete this rather uphill task. I was greeted by "you got it, you are almost there", "way to go champ", Amit clicking pictures and my daughter shouting 'mama' while I came biking into the transition area. I took around 2 hours and 5 minutes.

Transition 2: I placed my bike on the stand, removed my helmet and goggles, placed them on the mat and set off to complete my last division of the race. It was a 6.2 mile run. "You might finish it under four hours if you maintain that usual pace of yours," Amit remarked.

It took me not more than a couple of minutes to head out for that run.

Strides to the finish – The sun was shining down fiercely by this time. I set off on my run greeted by yet another hill at the beginning. However, this time, it failed to daunt me as being a runner primarily, I was used to running on hills as a part of my training regime. I had run at Stanford Dish a few times. It was the last leg of the race and the excitement levels were soaring. I was just 6 miles away from my goal, I thought and felt goosebumps just thinking about it. As I ran along the course, I bumped into a few participants who had cruised past me in the ocean. They smiled and I waved back. We hi-fived one another. This was the best part about sportsman spirit. Even in an event which appears like a solo sport, this sort of team support from your co-participants keeps you going even when your energy levels hit rock bottom. It was almost noon and my pace dropped significantly. I was going at a pace that I'd normally use for a heart rate based training run.

As I ran by the cliff, I noticed the beautiful view of the ocean below. I could see some surfers on the waves and the water looked so inviting at that time of the day. Part of me wished I could ditch my run and bask in the cool water instead. However, I had to keep going.

I finished two loops and was on my third loop. With every stride, I was edging closer to the finish line. I felt a pulsating rush through my veins as I ran past many runners. On the pavement, I saw a lot of people walking their dogs and they cheered us saying, "great going". It was tough to run without music but these cheers kept my energy levels boosted throughout. I soon reached the point where I was asked to turn right and enter the beach. I could spot the familiar arch to the finish line from where I was. It was at the far end of the beach. With the sun beating down in an unrelenting manner, I found it difficult to run on sand especially with shoes. I had half a mind to take off my shoes but seeing the sand glistening below, I decided against it. I'd probably burn my feet.

The beach had a typical ambience of a lazy Saturday afternoon. Families had spread their towels and were sunbathing. Some of them were surfing. There was music playing and it overall felt like a party place.

As I ran amidst the colourful towels, umbrellas and folks in their beach wear, hanging out at the beach with their children, they encouraged me, "You go girl. You got this one."

I felt like a champion hearing all the whistles and claps. Just a few metres away from home. I plodded on the sand like a tired farmer who had spent the entire day ploughing on the fields. I faintly heard the emcee's announcement stating, "finishing her first Olympic triathlon from Stanford," I looked up and saw the arch to the finish line which was just a few feet away.

This was it! I am almost there I thought! As I cruised

through the finish line and received my medal, my heart did a leap of joy. There was something special about crossing the finish line. That feeling of elation, jubilation and triumph. A sense of accomplishment and the fact that you had achieved something worthwhile. As I crossed the timing mat in 4:14:21, a volunteer removed my timing chip and garlanded the medal around my neck. I gazed at it in admiration. It was the most beautiful medal that I'd ever seen. Carved in a shape of a mermaid, it was mystical and ethereal. Her hair was designed in a manner that was flowing in loose waves like the ocean.

"Congrats Swe! You did it! Way to go!" Amit thumped me on my shoulder.

Suddenly I was hit by a wave of fatigue and my knee began to hurt. I swam, biked and ran through the pain. My knees were begging me to stay in one place. I plonked on the chair near the finish line while my daughter climbed on my lap and hugged me tight.

I had achieved my dream finally! Never in my wildest dreams did I think I'd do a triathlon so soon. I glanced at the medal again. I was officially a triathlete now and 'A Mighty Mermaid' as per the Mermaid Series name given to the Olympic distance participants. I clutched the medal feeling a flurry of emotions like tumultuous waves in the ocean. My face flushed in ecstasy. The fact I hadn't eaten anything since wee hours of the morning, barring Gu gels, didn't bother me.

As I staggered down the beach towards the transition area to collect my bike, I bumped into the race director.

"How did it go?" he asked.

"Oh great. I finished my first Olympic distance today and I'm elated."

"Congratulations!" he remarked.

"Thank you. It was a very well-organized event."

Just then Amit quipped saying how I had an accident a few days before.

The race director did a double take and looked at me in surprise. He then noticed my bandaged arm and knee.

"So, you ran the pain out."

I nodded.

"Well congratulations again," he said.

I thanked him and headed towards transition. I collected my bike and headed towards the car. Suddenly it struck me that Amit and Samara hadn't eaten anything.

"Did you guys eat?" I asked.

"Yes. Managed to grab something from a café while you were running. What about you Swe? You must be starving."

"Let's go home and order a take out," I replied.

"Are you sure?"

"Yes, let's go."

As we drove back, I asked myself as to why I was putting myself through so much torture. Was it worth it? Who was I doing this for? At that moment, a flashback of those events that had transpired at Stanford came flooding back to me.

There were times that I felt like a monk and a loner. However, when I crossed the finish line that day, I felt I was no longer alone. There were several smiling faces out there that made me feel I was not alone in my journey. Numerous eager faces were waiting to see me cross the finish line and congratulate me for my feat. No doubt they were strangers but that was the incredible part of life's journey where tryst with the unknown makes this ride really worthwhile.

It was worth being aloof from the community. The feeling of high from crossing the finish line of a triathlon was far higher than those pegs at Friday night socials. The adrenalin rush through your entire system felt like an electric current. This was only the beginning and I wanted more.

Chapter 10

Deciding to Take Another Plunge – Ironman 70.3

"The first step is clearly defining what it is you're after,
because without knowing that, you'll never get it."

– Halle Berry

It had been three weeks since I had finished my Olympic distance triathlon. The beautiful finisher's medal carved in the shape of a mermaid was placed on the medal hanger just above the television set. I sat on the sofa and stared at it. Yes, I had finally done something that I thought was beyond my reach. I had done it in tough conditions with a bruised arm and knee. So why wasn't I thrilled as I should have been? Why did I feel a strange void – an emptiness that I couldn't explain?

I got up and pranced around my living room. I had finished my swim and also a writing assignment for my creative writing course that was in full swing now. The clock on the wall displayed 5:00 pm. I made myself a cup of green tea, hoping to ease the restless bouts. I sat down again and took a sip. From the window, I could see little children playing in the courtyard. Their parents sat on colourful mats placed on the green lawn, chatting with one another amicably. I didn't feel like joining them. I was supposed to get some reading done for my creative writing class but I couldn't get myself to do anything. Except probably stare listlessly at my medal.

The triathlon season had ended and there was nothing to look forward to until next April which is when the season starts in the Bay area. Even though I had done only a couple of events, I was already hooked to this sport. I personally loved the challenge of training for three different disciplines at the same time which included swimming, biking and running. The adrenalin rush of crossing one hurdle after another during an event gave me a sense of accomplishment.

I glanced at the calendar on the study desk which was placed adjacent to a wall in one corner of the living room – October 27th, 2017. Four months since I moved to Stanford from India with my family. Training for a triathlon helped me fill the void that I was beginning to experience more often. Back in India, I was always on my toes. I missed my community especially since my inability to build a similar community bothered me. Most of them were subsumed in their domestic lives and I don't blame them considering they had toddlers to look after. However, the fact that other folks and their partners in my husband's batch seemed to have found friends quickly made me feel even more lonely. Was there something wrong with me? Was I not open or friendly enough? The same doubts that haunted me back in high school began to creep in slowly. I brushed them away, convincing myself that it was just my mind playing tricks with me. Maybe it was a phase when irrational thoughts clouded my sensibilities like a mist. Maybe I just need to give it more time. But how much more time?

I continued sipping my green tea. The aromatic ginger flavour wafted into my senses and I closed my eyes allowing my nerves to relish the feeling. It was just a matter of time before those thoughts made their way into my head again. A classic case of an idle mind being a devil's workshop. That's the reason why running and training for triathlons kept me sane. It channelized my negative thoughts into something purposeful.

Every time I crossed the finish line of a race and was garlanded the finisher's medal, I felt a sense of achievement. This elevated my confidence levels especially in a situation like this in a foreign country. It gave me an identity and made me feel worthwhile. An hour and a half had passed with my random musings. Amit would be home from class anytime now after picking up Samara.

Just then, I heard the sound of the key at the door as the locked turned.

"Hi mama," Samara called out excitedly.

"Hi Swe," Amit came in. "What's up?" he asked looking at my sullen face.

My empty cup was placed on the table. I was too lethargic to put it in the dishwasher. I stared at it as the merry laughter of the children playing outside drifted in.

"Nothing," I muttered moodily.

My husband looked confused, "Are you okay?"

I pointed to the mermaid medal and said, "What next?"

"What do you mean?"

"I mean what do I look forward to now?" I snapped.

"Well… there are lots of things happening. There is Halloween celebration at Stanford followed by cultural nights…."

"Sure. Halloween will be fun. But still… I need something to keep me going continuously. I mean something purposeful."

Samara had switched on the television and began watching *Ice Age Dawn of the Dinosaurs*. The character Sid was screaming in the background as he was being carried away by the mother dinosaur and I was on the verge of screaming myself. For a minute, I too wished that I was kidnapped by dinosaurs instead. That would be an interesting experience and an adventure.

"Look Amit. It has been four months. I have tried mingling with the community. I am not finding that many people I can connect with. Most of them are interested in either domestic chores, gossiping, shopping or partying. None of that interests me. In that case, I'd rather spend my time training, reading a book or writing. I came here to achieve a certain goal."

"Well you have achieved your goal."

"I want more. Ever since I finished my triathlon, I have been feeling a sense of void. I don't know why. I mean there is nothing now. I feel empty and feel like training for something. It just keeps me going. I just…" and burst into tears.

Samara looked at me curiously. I wiped my tears and gave her a weak smile. She turned her attention back to the television while Amit was trying to comprehend my situation.

"Okay. What is it you want to do?"

"I wish I knew," I sniffled.

Silence.

The dialogues from *Ice Age* were playing out loud and clear. The characters were cracking jokes and laughing like hyenas while I sullenly stared at the screen. It seemed like everyone in the world was happy except me, including fictional animated characters.

After a few minutes, Amit spoke up.

"Alright. Since we are here only till summer, why don't

you challenge yourself for something bigger before we go back home?"

"Like what?"

"Why don't you train for Ironman 70.3?"

It took a moment for his words to sink in. Wait a minute. Does he mean that gruelling endurance race that involved 1.2 miles swimming, 56 miles biking followed by 13.1 miles running? With those stringent cut-off times? No way.

"Are you kidding me?"

"Why not? I think you have the potential to do one."

"Hell no! That's beyond my reach."

"You seem restless and unsettled. Training for a shorter distance all these months kept you going. Training for this mammoth distance will take your mind off those nagging thoughts in your head. Think about it. I am sure there must be some Ironman event happening in the Bay area in summer."

"But...."

"Listen. Can you do a triathlon in India? Can you train for it? We don't have clean waters for open water swimming. Roads are terrible for cycling. No separate lanes. So many accidents. You won't get this opportunity again Swe."

He entered the kitchen to make some coffee. I thought about it for a while. The idea seemed tempting. The Ironman 70.3 title was a prestigious one. I remember when coach Viv, back in India, finished his first Ironman

70.3, the running community really respected and looked up to him. What an incredible feeling it must be to just cross the finish line of a race that tests human endurance levels. I imagined myself attaining the title and drifted away into a temporary dreamland until my logical side brought me back to reality.

I had just begun my triathlon journey. Was I aiming for something beyond my reach? I decided to talk to my coach first. I was perplexed and wanted some clarity. I looked at the clock. It was 7:30 pm Pacific time which was 8:00 am in India. I dialled Viv's number. He picked up after a few rings.

"Viv?"

"What's up?"

I decided to get straight to the point.

"Listen, I know I just did a couple of triathlon events. Now I am really hooked onto the sport. I can't wait for the next tri season to start. I know I can never do a triathlon in India. You know how the facilities are. I thought I should make the most of it while I am here. Amit just suggested that I should train for the Ironman 70.3. What do you think?"

A long pause.

I waited anxiously wondering what he'd say. The television was blaring loudly. Amit sat down next to me and took a sip of his coffee. I asked him to turn down the volume a bit.

After what seemed like eternity, Viv spoke.

"Yeah why not? I think you should go for it."

I literally yelped, "Are you sure? You don't think I am rushing into things or jumping distances too fast?"

"Which Ironman 70.3 are you targeting? When is the event?"

I grabbed my laptop from the table and browsed through the Ironman website. I looked eagerly for something around June or July. I saw an Ironman 70.3 scheduled in July. It was in Santa Rosa. Just a couple of hours drive from Stanford.

"Viv are you there?"

"Yes!"

"There is one on July 28th, Ironman 70.3 Santa Rosa."

"Yes, I am seeing that one too. I think you should go for it."

"Are you also checking the Ironman website?"

"Yeah. You have enough time. I will put you on your base building phase for the next three months. After that we can up your intensity."

"You really think I can do this?"

"Look. You are a decent swimmer and a runner. Yes, you can definitely work on your bike and I will help you with that."

I took a deep breath feeling a flurry of emotions – excitement, uncertainty and nervousness at the same time."

"Okay I will sign up for it. Thanks Viv."

"Sure."

It was already dark outside yet my evening suddenly became brighter. I had something to look forward to even though it was months away. I continued browsing the Ironman website, eager to learn about the events and the cities that they were being held at.

My attention fell on the event that was scheduled for September 9th, Ironman 70.3 Santa Cruz. Santa Cruz, I thought wistfully. How I wish I could do that one instead. Unfortunately, we would have left the country by then. I was familiar with the quaint town and Cowell Beach. I did my first Sprint distance triathlon in August there. Somehow it already felt like home.

"There is no chance that our stay will be extended, right?" I asked Amit who was watching the animation with my daughter.

He shook his head, "So, what did Viv say?"

"He said I should just go for it."

"See, I told you so. Now you have something to focus on besides your classes."

"I wish I could do Santa Cruz…," my voice trailed.

I diverted my mind and began to read about Ironman 70.3 Santa Rosa. The swim was in Lake Sonoma and the bike course was a hilly one amidst the vineyards. The run was along a creek and a flat course. I clicked on the link to register for the event and filled in my details. After entering my credit card details, I got a conformation mail. I was officially registered for the race.

An inexplicable strange feeling engulfed me. Would I be able to make it? Would I still manage to train, work on my class assignments and go for short vacations? It will definitely elevate my identity. What a privilege it will be if I actually cross the finish line of Ironman 70.3. It sure will eliminate the feeling that I am good for nothing. I will feel stronger, more confident about the fact that I have achieved something big. It will be an incredible tale to tell my grandchildren someday that I overcame a lot of insecurities to achieve this.

I liked challenges. I liked proving myself wrong and that my inhibitions were nothing but a figment of my warped-up imagination resulted from the ghosts of my past. The fact that I was plump and pudgy in school. The fact that I was taunted for it. The fact that it gave me a complex to never play any sport.

I had come a long way since then. Long enough to sign up for an endurance race. Ironman 70.3! Wow! Just the sound of it was enough to drift me into a trance. I closed my eyes and visualized myself, standing tall and proud as I crossed the finish line with my country's flag, tears of contentment pouring down my cheeks and basking in the happiness of my new-found identity – Ironman or rather Ironwoman!

I knew it was going to be a long and arduous journey. I resolved to get there even if it meant dealing with several hurdles that would come in the way of my dream.

Chapter 11

Crossing Various Hurdles

"Let it rain on some days,
Let yourself shiver on some cold nights,
So when it's Spring you'll know why
it was all worth going through."

– *Sanhita Baruah*

Training for Ironman 70.3 was no piece of cake. It almost felt like a full-time job. The training schedule given by Coach Viv had me gawking for a while before I put it in action. I thought back to the half marathon training plan that I had followed before venturing into triathlons. The half marathon training plan seemed like attending kindergarten in comparison to this Ironman 70.3 training plan. The weekly half marathon training plan included only one workout per day which was something like this.

Tuesdays included run speed intervals.

Wednesdays were allocated to either strength training or cross training like biking.

Thursdays involved a tempo run of 5 miles.

Fridays were reserved for strength training or swimming.

Saturdays included a 4-6 mile run.

Sundays were allocated for long runs and the distance was between 10-15 miles.

Mondays were for rest and recovery.

This was just a sample plan for a weekly base build-up training for the Ironman 70.3 race. The intensity increased by the week along with the mileages.

However, my plans were quite intense as devised by Coach Viv. Tuesday involved a 1.3 mile swim in the morning with few drills. The pull sets were to be done using a pull buoy. Kick sets were incorporated in the regime, which were to be done using a kickboard. It also involved a fast and slow swim in intervals. In the evening, I was to do bike intervals and the overall duration included an hour and ten minutes.

Wednesday was reserved for run speed intervals. It was the one minute fast run followed by one minute slow run. I had to repeat it 10 to 15 times. I used the same day for strength training in the gym.

Thursday included brick training. It was a 75 minute bike ride followed by 30 minutes of running.

Friday included another swim with drills. The distance ranged from 1-1.4 miles.

Saturday involved a two-three hour bike ride.

Sunday was reserved for another one mile swim followed by a 10 mile run.

My daily routine became even more hectic since the training mileages were longer. Also since the days were getting shorter due to the onset of winter, it was impossible to go for rides in the evenings. I didn't want to ride in the dark or in the rain that was expected during winters in California. So, when I spoke to Viv about this, he recommended that I get an indoor smart fitness bike trainer called the Wahoo Kickr Trainer. The technology allowed riders to get a feel of riding outdoors while sitting inside your homes. This was especially useful for those who can't venture outdoors either due to weather conditions or busy schedules. Viv convinced me stating that it was a good investment.

Amit helped me in looking out for a good trainer. We placed an order with another bike store in Palo Alto. He later helped me set it up. Considering I was pathetic with such things like setting up appliances, Amit's help came in handy. I also purchased a pull buoy set and a kickboard from Sports Basement Store – the same place from where I got my wetsuit and other swim stuff.

My routine continued like before. I had to get my workouts, household chores, writing assignments and reading done before Samara came home. I took some time getting used to biking on the trainer. It was very different from biking on the road. When I biked on the road, I was treated to a good amount of scenery which was an incentive to keep me going. Besides, seeing other bikers on the road kept me motivated. As I had mentioned before, it gave me a sense of freedom to whizz past the highways with the wind blowing on my face. Biking on the trainer was sort of stationary biking which isn't so much fun. I had to plug in music to stay motivated for those long biking sessions. However, this was really useful especially on the days that it rained. Amit was supportive on weekends especially when my workouts got demanding. On some Sundays, I would take part in some running event which ended up becoming my training run. Besides it gave me an opportunity to explore different places and get a feel of running events in California. The spirit and atmosphere was just amazing.

My diet was the same as before except that it involved slightly larger portions. The demanding regime had increased my appetite. The day would start with a peanut butter sandwich accompanied by fruits which were usually strawberries. Lunch was lentils and green veggies. Sometimes it would be grilled salmon with quinoa. Snacks involved a fistful of dry fruits, fruits and green tea. Dinner was similar to lunch. There were times when I would do a take out if I was too exhausted to cook a meal. Since my meals contained a lot of the essential protein, carbohydrates, fibre and other vitamins, I did not feel the need to consume additional supplements.

For the initial two months of November and December, I was pumped up and charged. It was hectic but at least it kept those bouts of loneliness at bay. The training left me with no time to ponder about anything or anyone. I soon distanced myself from the business school community and lived in my own world of swims, bikes and runs. I no longer felt compelled to attend social dos or gatherings where I had to force myself to make small talk with people who did not matter to me or who mostly looked through me.

Besides my training, I spent a lot of time reading since I had access to the Stanford libraries. Reading also calmed me down. Exploring different genres and writing styles also enabled my learning curve as a student of creative writing.

I got a break from my training during the Thanksgiving break which was around the end of November. During my two-week Christmas vacation at Hawaii, I managed to incorporate my training by using the hotel gym and pool. The only thing I missed was biking. However, I knew that I could make up the missed sessions once I got back to my Stanford accommodation.

January 2018 started off on a sweet note by taking part in the Hot Chocolate Run at San Francisco. It was inside the Golden Gate Park which was beautiful and scenic. It was a 9.4 mile run and I finished it in a strong manner.

My training sessions was making me stronger by the day. Everything was going well until that fateful day when I succumbed to an awful injury.

It was just a week after the Hot Chocolate Run. I was at the gym and had just finished my run speed intervals on the treadmill. On the same day, I was doing few leg strengthening exercises. One of the exercises involved step ups. I had to step up on a bench and step down. At one point, I stepped on a dumbbell which was placed carelessly by another member. Since I didn't see it, I slipped and fell down badly. For a minute, everything around me whirled. My head was spinning and my left ankle was hurting. A couple of gym members rushed to my side and the person at the counter came up to me.

"Are you okay girl?" asked the person at the front desk.

"No, I am not. Can't you see? Some moron left that dumbbell lying on the floor. It rolled out and I didn't even see it coming. Maybe you need to put up a notice saying, 'All dumbbells need to be racked back on the shelf'," I retorted. Along with the pain, I felt a surge of anger. I was angry at that careless soul who had caused this injury.

The person backed off in alarm.

"Huh... sorry about that...."

"Well you better be. I am training for Ironman 70.3. Look what has happened now."

"Calm down. Maybe you need some ice?"

I got up and my ankle hurt as though someone had sliced it with a knife. I picked up the dumbbells and threw the person a defiant look as I continued my exercise.

"I need no ice. What you all need is a bit of common sense."

The members around me looked as though they had been hit by a tornado. Their faces went pale and they tried reassuring me. However, for some reason, the pain aggravated my temper. I continued my workout and threw them another look.

"You see nothing is gonna break me. You keep that ice. I am going to make a complaint."

They stood there helplessly and then dispersed rather hesitatingly. Probably wondering if they were dealing with a mad woman. Well I was certainly mad. Mad because I had expected certain gym etiquettes to be followed like placing the weights on the rack. Failure to do so would cause an injury to another person. Like what happened to me. When I finished my workout, I registered a complaint at the front desk and also with the manager.

By now my left ankle had swollen. It looked as though someone had stuffed a tennis ball inside it. I was limping and frustrated. I felt like I was in a snakes and ladders board game. Just as my fitness was peaking and I felt I was almost close to the goal, I had to be swallowed by this enormous serpent and that pushed me back to where

I had started. I decided to not waste time and headed to see the doctor.

At Palo Alto Medical Foundation, I met the emergency doctor who gave me ibuprofen to ease the pain and advised icing my ankle. She asked me to fix an appointment with the physiotherapy department. While I was able to swim and bike, I couldn't run for a month. It was disheartening especially since my running form was hitting its peak. I reduced my diet significantly for fear of putting on weight. I just had fruits for breakfast, vegetables and lentils for lunch and dinner. I cut out my peanut butter sandwich, fish and quinoa out completely. It led to some bouts of irritability. I found myself snapping at Amit and Samara. They were both quite patient and understanding, realising that I was going through a bad phase.

Eliminating running was like eliminating a big chunk of fitness in my life. I continued my swims and biking. Sometimes I'd end up using the cross trainer at the gym and substitute it for running. My complaint was taken seriously and they had put up a notice stating that all dumbbells should be racked. The manager apologized for what happened and empathized with me. He said it was just a matter of time and the injury would heal.

When I spoke to Viv, he was empathetic. He cut down my running sessions from the training schedule. He checked if I was allowed to bike and swim. I answered in affirmative. So, my tryst with swim and bike continued until March. After a few sessions with the physiotherapist, my ankle had healed. Running was incorporated into my training regime again. I participated in the Santa Cruz Half Marathon on March 4th. It was a beautiful and a scenic run which took me on a trail. The run ended on Cowell Beach which was the same place where I had come for my open water swim. I felt a sense of nostalgia when I stood on the sands and gazed at the ocean. Only later did I realize that running this half marathon actually came in handy at the right time.

I also did an Olympic distance duathlon at this place called Morgan Hill. Morgan Hill was situated about forty-five minutes away from Stanford. It was a scenic town. The beautiful greenery cascading along the mountains reminded me of Switzerland. This event was conducted by USA Productions – one of the largest event management companies that conducted triathlons and running events. There were no cut-off times for this event as they wanted every participant to finish the race. I decided to take part in the duathlon which involved a run followed by a bike ride and ended with another short run.

The distance involved a 6.2 mile run followed by 25 miles biking and a 3.1 mile run. The bike course was extremely hilly. At one point, I had to walk my bike at this steep hilly section after which it was all downhill. Despite this, I discovered that I had cut down my bike timing by fifteen minutes compared to the previous Olympic distance triathlon. Not bad I thought. "Well done Rocky," I hugged my bike and lifted it in elation. Overall, I had finished the race in 3:29:41. I was inching towards my goal once again.

My fitness picked up slowly at the onset of spring. April started off with a bang. I participated in an event which involved a 60 mile bike ride on Saturday and a 13.1 mile run on Sunday. This was at a place called Fresno which was three hours from Stanford. We drove there on Friday. Saturday morning turned out to be rainy. I had never ridden in the rains but seeing the spirit of my co-participants, I decided to go ahead. In the pelting rain and chanting my mantra *Om Gan Ganapathaye Namaha*, I whizzed past the freeways, orange orchards and finally finished my bike ride in four hours. This was my longest distance on the bike and I was relieved that I hadn't encountered a flat tyre. Sunday turned out to be a sunny day and the run took us through the zoo. For the first time during my run, I saw elephants, lions and giraffes. It was an exhilarating experience. Most importantly this weekend gave me immense confidence of conquering the Ironman 70.3 race in July.

I did my second Olympic distance triathlon at Half Moon Bay which was about thirty minutes away from Stanford. This event was also organized by USA Productions and had no cut-off times. Like every other Olympic distance, this involved a 0.95 mile swim, 25 miles biking and 6.2 miles running. I had an opportunity to attend a swim clinic which was conducted for one day. It would help me acquaint myself with the open waters again. It was at the Half Moon Bay swim clinic where I met Coach Jay and his daughter Emily. I still remember that day clearly. I had a squeamish feeling just looking at the ocean. Coach Jay put me at ease with his warm smile. His daughter Emily was assisting him. As we headed towards the beach, I heard a couple of locals mention that the water here was really cold. When I put my feet to test the temperature, it felt like I had stepped on a glacier. I shivered despite wearing a wetsuit. As we all entered the water, we warmed up initially to acclimatize our body to the temperature. The race director Ryan Coelho was on his kayak. Emily entered the water with us as Coach Jay was nursing an injury. I tried putting my head down and succeeded only for a few yards. After that I resorted to my usual style of sticking my head out and paddling. I noticed others whizz past me. I expressed my concern to Emily stating how I panicked on seeing other people go faster than me. She reassured me that it was my race and I need not be bogged down by the speed of other participants. It was then that I was reminded of the mantra that I usually followed – the only competition is with yourself.

We did a couple of laps in the water. After that Emily came up to me and said I was doing fine. "You should learn to trust yourself. You were doing good."

I was grateful for her encouraging words and also struck by her humility. When I later learnt that she was a podium finisher at several triathlon races, I looked at her in awe. People who display humility despite their remarkable achievements earned my respect instantly. It takes a really secure person to have their head on their shoulders. Considering that I had come across several people with a chip on their shoulder this last one year, meeting people like Penni, Coach Char, Emily and Coach Jay felt like a breath of fresh air.

Coach Jay and Emily were a part of a group called PacWest Endurance. They conducted training camps for Ironman 70.3 events. I was thrilled to hear that they were conducting a training camp at Santa Rosa in July. I went home happier thinking that I was slowly inching towards my Ironman 70.3 goal. I finished my Olympic distance triathlon at Half Moon Bay in 4:04:41. Despite a bad swim, I had still managed to shave off ten minutes from my previous Olympic distance triathlon race at the mermaid series in October. My biking especially had gotten stronger thanks to those months of hard work. My bike Rocky, true to its name, stood by me like a rock and ensured my journey was a smooth one.

My training continued. Viv had upped my intensity from end of April. The mileages in the swim, bike and run had increased by large margins. One Sunday involved a Sprint distance triathlon which was 0.45 miles swimming,

12.5 miles biking and 3.1 miles running. I swam at the Stanford pool wearing my tri-suit, immediately hopped on my bike and did a few loops around campus till my accommodation. Then I parked my bike inside my house and ran around the campus.

I did my third Olympic distance triathlon in June end, just before my birthday. I swam 0.95 miles, biked 25 miles and ran 6.2 miles. It was again organized by USA Productions with no cut-off times. It took place at Pleasanton which was situated in the East Bay that was about an hour from the Stanford Campus. Even though the swim was in a lake, I found myself getting exhausted. The water was much warmer than any of the other places where I had done my triathlons. Being peak summer, my energy levels were drained. I began to ignore the signals that my body was giving me. I blamed it on the heat and continued pushing throughout the bike ride which was hilly. The run was on a trail where I ended up walking half the time. Nevertheless, I finished the race and clutched the finisher's medal – a birthday gift to myself. Little did I realize that this birthday present would be a nail in the coffin. Fatigue had begun to make its way into my body. I brushed it off as an effect of the heat.

A month was left now for the race. The Ironman 70.3 training camp organized by Coach Jay at Santa Rosa was next weekend. If the camp goes well, then I'd soon earn the title of Ironman. And again, just as I was inching towards my goal, I was encountered with yet another serpent at the Santa Rosa Camp. It felt like I was in a never-ending snakes and ladders game.

Chapter 12

Heading Towards A Dead End

"Sometimes life seems a dark tunnel with no light at the end,
but if you just keep moving forward, you will end up
in a better place."

– Jeffrey Fry

The camp at Santa Rosa almost made me give up my dream of Ironman 70.3.

It was the first week of July and the temperature was close to 100 degree Fahrenheit. It was so hot that I could have probably cooked a meal out there on the roads without a gas stove. The sun was beating down fiercely. Santa Rosa looked dry and haggard. The trees seem to be drooping and everything around sported a shade of pale yellow. I landed there on Friday evening along with my husband and daughter. Checking into the Astro Motel Downtown, I later met Coach Jay and others who had signed up for the camp.

Coach Jay headed a group called PacWest Endurance where he coached and trained triathletes. The group organized triathlon camps in different parts of California just a month before a major event. It was a sort of course preview for the participants where they actually get to swim, bike and run on the designated race course. Having signed up for Ironman 70.3 Santa Rosa, I decided to attend this camp. There were totally eight of us including the people from the PacWest team. A brief round of introductions was done. I learnt that this was the first attempt at Ironman 70.3 for most of them. However, they had been biking for years and had gone as far as 100 miles during their rides. In a triathlon, the major portion was spent on the bike. So, if you are a strong biker, half the battle is won.

I dispelled the nervous thoughts as Coach Jay began to speak. He gave us a briefing about the itinerary of the camp.

"We are going to be swimming 1.2 miles at Lake Sonoma, bike 56 miles and run at least 5-6 miles this weekend," he said. "So, let us meet at the lobby at 6:30 am sharp. We load our bikes in the van and drive to Lake Sonoma," he continued. The rest of us nodded in affirmative.

I woke up Saturday morning with knots in my stomach. To me, this camp seemed like a do or die situation. I just had a month left in the Bay area to fulfil my Ironman dream.

I thought about the day ahead. I'd probably be slowest amongst the pack on the bike. Considering that my swim still needed work, I'd be slow here as well. Amit and Samara were still fast asleep and I didn't have the heart to wake them up. I gathered my bag which I had packed the night before, containing my wetsuit, towel, goggles, swim cap and helmet. Putting on my tri-suit and a T-shirt, I wheeled my bike outside and closed the door gently.

The others had already gathered outside and were loading their bikes in the van.

"Why don't you grab a cup of coffee before we leave?" Coach Jay said.

I shook my head. Coffee would probably want to make me puke considering how squeamish I was already feeling. My body was feeling stiff and I kept chewing my fingernails. Swallowing repeatedly, I looked at the rest of the group. They were all subsumed in checking their bags to ensure they hadn't missed anything. Most of us seem to be on the same boat, yet it felt like I was the one drowning in a pool of despair.

The drive to Lake Sonoma was a bumpy one with several twists and turns. After about 30-35 minutes, I found myself facing the pristine body of blue water. So, this was the famous Lake Sonoma which was apparently a favourite amongst many triathletes. I had overheard some of them talk about it at the triathlon event in Pleasanton last week. They were discussing how heavenly it was to swim here amidst such clear turquoise blue waters. I gazed at the calm sheet of blue that sparkled in the sunlight, hoping that it won't give me a hard time as the ocean did. I slipped into my wetsuit and entered the lake along with the others.

"The water feels good, it's quite warm," remarked Trish. She had friendly blue eyes and a golden mass of curls that was now tucked inside a purple swim cap. She was part of the PacWest team. The lake definitely felt a lot warmer than Cowell Beach, shuddering as I recollected my first open water swim. I took a few laps to warm up.

The water was much calmer as compared to the ocean. Swimming in a lake should have felt like swimming laps in a pool. Yet my body experienced a strange sense of exhaustion that morning. I began to feel out of breath with just a couple of laps. It felt as though I was carrying a huge load on my back and swimming. My muscles were pleading me to stop much to my chagrin especially since I had just finished an Olympic distance triathlon last week. This time I wasn't even close to my menstrual cycle when my body developed a similar sort of fatigue.

Dismissing it off as just a nervous feeling, I swam towards the shore and assembled with the others around Coach Jay. He split us into two groups. The first group was to swim the entire 1.2 miles while another guy and I would be swimming close to the shore under Coach Jay's supervision. The first group took off like a school of fish while I waddled like a duck near the shore. I swam few laps again and Coach Jay tried to correct my strokes.

"I need you to lift your elbow up and slice your fingers into the water as though you are cutting it with a knife," he instructed. "That way you'll go faster."

I tried following his instructions but it was the case of old habits die hard. I had gotten used to a particular way of swimming and it was now difficult to incorporate a new technique. The other guy swimming along with me was really fast. I marvelled at his ability to swim strong strokes especially when he had just begun his triathlon journey a few months ago. I consoled myself saying that each person's journey and potential was different.

I then tried to focus on my strokes. My arms began to feel tired and worn out. I was going out of breath. By trying to go faster, I was actually fighting the water which drained my energy reserves. I swam back to the shore and told Coach Jay that I was done with the swim. He looked at me with a quizzical expression asking me if I was sure. He agreed albeit reluctantly when I nodded in affirmative. I noticed a trace of worry cloud his usually calm face when he asked me to relax.

Meanwhile, others were back from their swim. Apparently, they didn't swim the entire 1.2 miles but just around a mile. We trudged up along the steep slope from the lake, dripping wet from the swim. The parking lot was supposed to be the transition area where our bikes would be placed on race day. Slipping out of our wetsuits, buckling our helmets and putting on our gloves, we checked our bike tyres for air pressure. Coach Jay paired us up depending on our respective paces on the bike. The fastest were ahead of the pack while the slowest would trail behind. Coach Jay was to stop at all the turns in his van and ensure that we don't lose our way.

"If you are in any kind of trouble, take down my number and feel free to call me," he said.

Jotting down his number, I placed my phone on the holder in between my handlebars and began to follow the pack.

It was an initial downhill for a while before the gradual ascent began. I pedalled hard to keep myself moving up those inclines. The leaders of the pack had been well within my sight. Now I saw them move further away until they became a tiny speck. My quads were crying in pain and my lungs felt on fire. The boiling weather made it even worse. I wanted to quit at the 10th mile but kept going remembering my Ironman dream. My legs began to give up with every mile. The ascent wasn't getting easier and the weather hotter.

It felt as though someone had stabbed my back repeatedly. The excruciating pain lingered on throughout the bike ride. I stopped midway and looked around. I was surrounded by beautiful vineyards. Yet my eyes could not register the beauty of the contours of green that cascaded down the slopes. All that plagued my mind was that I wanted to survive this bike ride. I took a sip of water from the bottle that was racked on the stem of the bike. Feeling a teeny weenie better, I began to pedal again, bracing myself for those inclines. Chalk Hill Road was yet to come.

Around the 20th mile, I spotted Coach Jay's SAG vehicle. He stopped me and asked if I was doing okay. I almost said no when I remembered the Ironman 70.3 dream. I'd never get this chance again considering I was leaving California in the first week of August. He looked at my face and then at the bike.

"Have you been fitted on your bike?" he asked.

I looked at him quizzically wondering what that meant.

"When you get your bike, you need to ensure you get fitted on it."

At that point it almost made me feel as though my bike was some sort of a bridal outfit.

"I think so coach," without much thought I mumbled.

"Okay, but do go back again to the place where you got your bike from and ask them to get you fitted. They will adjust your seat and align your handlebars in a way which will prevent you from feeling any pain."

I thought I had done that when I initially got my bike. No wonder my back felt as though I had been carrying a sack of bricks, I deliberated. I made a mental note to do that when I got back to Stanford.

"What about your nutrition?" he looked at me kindly.

"Hmm I have water," I said.

"Water isn't going to be enough. You need something more like an energy drink and some energy bars."

I made another mental note to stock up on my nutrition.

"You are riding 56 miles and it is not an easy feat. You have to fuel up at regular intervals. Here have some Gatorade."

I gulped some down my parched throat. Feeling instantly better, I said I was ready to go. He made Tuan accompany me. The leaders of the pack were nowhere in sight. After a few yards, I was getting roasted in the unrelenting summer heat. I was nearing the major climb at Chalk Hill Road. There were ranches on either side with some houses. A dog suddenly barked and I was startled. I almost fell off from my bike. The ascent wasn't getting easier.

My breathing had become rapid and fast. It felt like someone had put a huge rock on my lungs. My calves felt as though they were being pulled back by reins. My pace had considerably slowed down. Around the 30th mile, I stopped and got off my bike. Tuan looked at me in surprise. I shook my head and stood there watching few cars whizz past the road. I observed other bikers breeze through the hills. Why couldn't I be like them, I wondered miserably. They had the will of an iron while I was nothing less than a chicken for surrendering to fatigue. My body refused to function anymore. All I wanted was to go lie down on a cosy bed in an air-conditioned room and get a good sleep.

"Are you sure you cannot go any further? We are almost up there, after that it is all downhill," Tuan tried to encourage me.

I looked up the hills which appeared like a Tsunami of a mountain. Just the thought of having to pedal up those inclines petrified me. I shook my head.

"Okay pull over to the other side and sit down there. I'll call Coach Jay."

I wheeled my bike across the road and sat down on the pavement. Tuan was calling Coach Jay while I watched a car go by. It was a white Honda Civic. It initially appeared so huge and then disappeared as a tiny speck until it was gone. My Ironman 70.3 dream faded away just like that until it was out of sight. I had entered this dark tunnel of doom realizing that there would be no light for a long time. I burst into tears. I felt betrayed by my bike for some reason. While Rocky had stood by me all this while, it refused to come to my aid when I needed it the most.

Tuan saw me and said, "I empathize with what you are feeling. I have been through this. Doing 70.3 is not easy. I have also struggled and in fact I failed to make the swim cut-off once."

"Really?" I looked at Tuan. He looked so strong and athletic that I couldn't imagine someone like him not making the swim cut-off.

"Yes, it happens. Some things are not in your control."

I listened intently, partly comforted by the fact that even good athletes go through a rough patch. Who was I to complain in that case?

I was almost blinded by the sun's rays despite wearing my glasses. The oppressive weather stifled me and I felt like being locked up in an oven. Just then I noticed Coach Jay's vehicle. Tuan loaded our bikes and I sat in the front next to Coach Jay. I was feeling ashamed wondering what he'd think of me. It almost took me back to my high school days when I feared facing my teacher after doing badly in a test. What if they lost respect for me, I'd wonder.

Coach Jay looked at me with concern, "What happened? You were doing fine."

I told him about how tired I was feeling and how I found it tough to bike on those inclines.

"I had no idea that the bike course was going to be this tough. I guess I'm not used to biking on hills." I paused as reality struck me just then.

I had to give up my dream. Ironman 70.3 was not for someone as average as me. What was I thinking? I was aiming for the moon when my place was just on the earth. Ironman 70.3 is for those athletes who were strong and confident. I had no athletic background to speak of. I was a plump kid who hated outdoors. And deep down that's who I'll always be irrespective of how many half marathon events or Olympic distance triathlons I do.

Uttering these words and taking this decision was probably one of the toughest things that I had done. Tougher than biking up those hills in the heat.

"Coach...," I began, "I don't think I'll do the 70.3 race end of this month. I mean, I thought I could when I signed up for it. But I didn't realize that the course was going to be so tough."

A wave of emotions washed over me. A sinking feeling that I let go of my dream. Slight relief that I don't have the pressure anymore. Maybe life could go back to normal without all those crazy training regimes. Right now, I wanted a break. I was anxious about what I'd tell Amit. Both Samara and he had sacrificed their weekend to come all the way here to support me. I felt I had let them down. I felt I had let Coach Viv down, who spent his time chalking out training plans for me.

Coach Jay's voice suddenly interrupted my thoughts.

"I think you have taken the right decision. It is not easy training for courses like these as they demand a great deal of time. You have just begun your tri journey. In another few months, you'll be strong enough to do Ironman 70.3."

"Yes, Coach I'll work hard. I'll do Olympic distances till then."

"I can help you with your training. What you need to do is figure out your nutrition. Consider switching over to cleats on your bike. That will help you especially on these inclines."

"I am unfortunately leaving in the first week of August."

"Oh!" he turned to look at me.

Silence filled the van as I experienced another sinking feeling. I had a chance to improve my triathlon skills in California. What a pity that I won't be staying back. Where would I have such opportunities in India? I blinked my tears and tried to change the topic by asking about how Trish and the others were doing.

Meanwhile we reached the hotel as the camp was done for the day. It was almost two in the afternoon. Coach Jay had organized a dinner in the evening. In the meantime, I wheeled my bike to my room which was on the first floor. I knocked on the door and Amit opened it smilingly. "We were just waiting for you." Samara squealed in delight. Looking at their happy faces, I wondered how I'd break my news to them.

As I sat down on the chair, Amit spoke excitedly, "Guess what? I got an email last night about an offer to work here in the Bay area. Looks like we will be here for some more time."

"Are you serious?" I asked in disbelief. "How come? I mean that is great."

"Yeah! I'll have to set up a venture fund for an Indian company and they are looking for someone to operate out of the US market."

"Nice!" My head felt dizzy as though I had just got out from one of those deadly rollercoaster rides at the theme parks. I felt this sudden wave of emotions wash over me. Similar to the one that I felt when I told Coach Jay that I was giving up my Ironman 70.3 dream. I looked up at Amit wondering how to break the news to him.

"So how did the camp go? All set to become Ironwoman?" he asked.

Samara came and sat on my lap. Instinctively she wrapped her tiny arms around me and planted a kiss on my cheek. I hugged her back, using all the comfort I could get from her warm cuddles. I rocked her gently and was soon lost in my thoughts. I wanted to make my family proud. I wanted to tell myself that I too was capable of achieving something. All these months of hard work towards a goal that I cherished was washed away in a jiffy. Did I rush into signing up for Ironman 70.3? When Amit suggested it few months back, I was confident of finishing the Ironman 70.3. My confidence soared in April when I did that 56 mile bike ride followed by 13.1 mile run at Fresno. I had felt so strong back then. Today my body felt overpowered by fatigue. I wasn't sure if it would even return to its old self.

"Hello, anyone home?" Amit tapped my shoulder lightly.

I jolted back to reality and looked at his concerned face for a long time before I could speak. Taking a deep breath, I finally managed to utter those words for the second time that day with an equally heavy heart.

"Amit, I am not doing the Ironman 70.3 race."

Silence filled the room. I could hear the birds chirping outside and the distant sound of the vehicles on the road streamed in. The outside world was moving on at a rapid pace while mine had come to a standstill. Samara was playing with my hair, oblivious to the tension that had gripped me. My eyes brimmed with tears as I uttered those words.

Amit came over to me and put an arm around my shoulder, "Hey, are you okay? What happened?"

The barrage of waterworks wouldn't stop and I cried nonstop much to the bewilderment of my family. Samara looked at me quizzically with her big black eyes. She wiped my tears gently while Amit stroked my head.

"The bike course was so hilly. I never anticipated it to be so hilly," I sniffled. "I mean I have biked on rolling hills at Half Moon Bay but this route has monstrous inclines. I quit halfway. And the heat was unbearable. I don't think I am ready Amit. I think I rushed into it. I...."

He handed me a bottle of water. I drank it and felt slightly better.

Taking another deep breath, I continued, "I don't know what would have happened if I didn't come to this camp. I would have struggled on race day and not reached the finish line. That would have been such a humiliation. I had a word with Coach Jay. I think I will have to postpone it to next year. My body is just gone... I am feeling so exhausted. I mean I just couldn't push today."

Amit looked at me for a long time, compassion oozing out of his brown eyes. They had a tinge of sadness in them. "You do have the potential to do Ironman 70.3. You have just over trained and tired yourself by doing those multiple events."

"I don't. I thought I could but the reality hit me at today's camp. I am not meant for something like Ironman 70.3."

"Swe, I know your strength. You have great endurance and tremendous potential. Kudos to you for even biking half the distance in this heat. It is really hot out there. Samara and I went to the park next door and we came back in 15 minutes. She couldn't bear the heat."

I listened and was partially relieved to hear that it wasn't just me who found the weather to be brutal.

"I feel terrible. I mean I made you guys come all the way. I worked hard all these months and... I know it is the right decision. I don't want to go to the race and flop. And what about the hotel reservation? Can we cancel it?"

For the first time that afternoon, I saw traces of anxiety on Amit's face. His usually calm face appeared troubled.

He took his phone and scrolled down his email. Punching a few numbers, he called up Marriot Courtyard where he had made a reservation for four days prior to the race. After he made enquiries, he hung up with a worried expression on his face.

He sat down on the bed burying his face in his palms. Alarmed, I set Samara down in a jiffy.

"What happened?" I asked, my chest tightening into several knots.

"I made a blunder. I booked the rooms without any refund. Now if I cancel, I lose the money."

It felt as though someone had sliced my heart with a sword. My head throbbed and it wasn't just from the summer heat. Samara was watching few videos on the mobile, engulfed in her world of *Peppa Pig*. At that moment, I longed to go back to my childhood where I had nothing to worry about.

I felt even worse than I had at the camp. Because of me, Amit would lose the money and I probably wouldn't even get a refund of the registration fees for the Ironman 70.3. I had wasted everyone's time and money. How I wish I could turn the clock back in time and change certain things. I knew I couldn't and here I was facing a rather grave situation.

Time ticked away as I stared at the walls wondering what to do. Finally, I managed to break that deafening silence. "We are all meeting for dinner later this evening.

Shall I try asking them? Maybe they might know someone who would be interested."

Amit nodded half-heartedly. As sunny as it was outside, the ambience couldn't have been gloomier inside. Samara was oblivious to the sombre atmosphere and kept looking at our faces smilingly. After a few hours, we got ready to meet others for dinner.

Everyone had gathered around the lobby of the motel first. Coach Jay had a brief meeting and a recap of today's events. He asked each of us to voice out what we felt. When my turn came, it took every ounce of courage to admit that I wasn't going ahead with the 70.3 race, much to their surprise. I said I wasn't just ready and that I'd like to train more before I take that plunge. At this moment, I took the opportunity to put in a word about the hotel scenario. To which everyone said they would let me know in a week.

The camp was a humbling experience. It gave me a chance to reflect on my goals, strengths and weaknesses. It was a tough albeit a right decision. Better quit now than not making it to the finish line on race day. The first thing that I did after getting back to Stanford was to get my bike fitted as Coach Jay had suggested. The toughest part was explaining my decision to Coach Viv who was very understanding.

"One day I'll make you proud Coach. I feel so bad that I have let you down," I told him miserably. I kicked myself for not being able to achieve my goal. I felt guilty as Viv had spent months in designing a training plan for me.

He was empathetic yet practical.

"You need to make yourself feel proud. It is ultimately your race and your decision. Don't worry. You will do a 70.3 race soon."

The football world cup in July was the only silver lining in the dark cloud that had descended over me. Seeing those high scoring games and some players in action kept my spirits up. It was the most entertaining world cup considering some of the antics displayed by few players. It took away my mind from the Ironman 70.3 race for some time. Watching any sport on television was always therapeutic. Seeing the professional athletes in action gave me the adrenalin rush that I couldn't experience from any event that month. I was asked by my coach to not exert myself and to recover from fatigue and stress.

I used this time to connect with my old Coach Rama who had been conducting boot camp sessions for me in Mumbai until he migrated to Canada in 2015. He was from the army background and very sensible. He comforted me saying that I had probably trained too hard and asked me to take rest. I spoke to Ashok Someshwar – another mentor of mine from Mumbai Road Runners. He was empathetic and lent a patient ear. He too assured me that I was capable of doing the Ironman 70.3 race someday. I was grateful for his words of encouragement at a time when I was feeling such lows.

There were still no takers for our hotel since we had booked it for four days. After a lot of deliberation, we decided to use this opportunity as a short vacation to the wine country. It was a much needed one, considering the amount of stress we had undergone the past couple of months. Little did I realize that this vacation would be a turning point in my life. There was an unexpected surprise that awaited me.

Chapter 13

Vacation with A Twist

*"There are no wrong turnings. Only paths we had
not known we were meant to walk."*

— *Guy Gavriel Kay, Tigana*

Vacation in the wine country turned out to be much better than I had expected. It was slated to be a relaxed break where I would come back with renewed vigour. And I did!

After checking into our hotel on Wednesday, we headed straight to the wineries. Tasting different kinds of wine and learning about the grapes took my mind away from the Ironman stress. After a long time, I was actually savouring the present moment instead of worrying about the future. It was interesting to learn about something new other than swimming, biking and running. I sat there in the wine tasting room and watched the sky turn a radiant shade of orange. Samara was sipping her orange juice while sketching on a piece of paper. Amit was also enjoying his wine. The atmosphere was peaceful and pleasant. The cloud of turmoil that had engulfed my mind was gradually beginning to dissipate.

However, on Thursday morning, when I saw few strong looking athletes check into the hotel with their bikes, my heart sank. It felt as though someone had punched my stomach. I stood there looking at them. They had a surety about them while they wheeled their bikes. Their confident demeanour suggested that it was probably not their first time. They would have earned several such Ironman 70.3 medals. This was just another race for them. Amit and Samara were standing by the reception area, talking to the staff and finding out about things to do. I continued gaping at the athletes who were streaming in. I walked up to one of them remarking, "Nice bike." It instantly broke the ice and the man smiled. He looked in his 50s, athletic and tall.

"Thanks," he grinned.

"So, is this the first time you are doing this race?" I asked.

"Oh no. I have done this for a few years now."

"Wow. So how do you find the course?"

"It's pretty okay. Just a little steep portion at Chalk Hill Road. Otherwise it is a good course."

I nodded, "Yes, I found that tough too."

"So, you are doing the race?" he asked.

"No! I had attended the camp and found the bike course gruelling. I had signed up for it but I guess I am not ready. So I decided to quit."

He gave me a sympathetic look. "Well I hope you do this next year," he remarked.

"Hope so too. Good luck to you."

"Thanks," he smiled.

I experienced a weird mix of emotions. All this while, I was petrified of the water. Now I had one more fear that I had to overcome – biking on the hills. For a moment, I felt useless standing there, watching all those athletes walking in, sure of crossing the finish line. A little voice told me that this race was meant for experienced athletes and not a novice like me. Using that as a comfort blanket, I kept telling myself the same thing that entire day.

When Amit and Samara came up to me, he remarked that it was probably a good idea for me to not go ahead with the race.

"Those athletes look like they have been training for years. Give yourself time."

Feeling a sudden wave of misery, I walked quietly up to the Charles Schutz Museum. Learning about the cartoonist who created the *Peanuts* cartoon characters, made me feel a lot better. I cheered up on seeing the caricatures of Snoopy, Woodstock, Charlie Brown and his friends. As a little girl, I had watched the cartoon

Snoopy Come Home several times. It was nice to revisit my childhood again. Later that afternoon, we visited the Ironman Village.

The Ironman Village was just a 10-minute walk from our hotel. It was an expo where the registered participants collected their bib, timing chip, swim cap, T-shirt and few goodies. There were stalls that sold some merchandise which included tri-suits, wetsuits, bike gear, running T-shirts that had Ironman 70.3 written on it with the Ironman logo. I went there and collected my T-shirt and told the volunteers with a heavy heart that I wasn't doing the event. I had in the meantime mailed the organizers asking them to withdraw my name. I received more sympathetic looks that day which made me feel worse. Feeling like I had failed an important examination, I walked out of the expo.

Amit pulled me to check the merchandise. I looked at some of the tri-suits displayed. A particular one with a mix black and fluorescent green caught my eye. It had Ironman written on it. I took it, placed it on myself and glanced at it in the mirror. It looked great but I didn't deserve it, I thought wistfully.

"That's a nice looking tri-suit. Would look great on you," a lady smiled.

I smiled back grateful for her kind words. It appeared as though the universe was conspiring to send kind hearted people my way, in order to cheer me up.

"I think you should take it. You anyways wanted to buy a new one," Amit remarked.

"Should I?" I asked hesitatingly.

"Yeah! Just try it on. If it fits you, take it."

"Where is Samara?"

Just then I spotted her checking out the mugs that read Ironman.

She accompanied me to the changing room. The suit fitted me so I ended up purchasing it along with a matching vizer cap. Little did I realize that I'd consider myself worthy of this tri-suit in the next couple of months.

The entire Friday was spent exploring trails and the redwood trees. The woods had a calming effect. I was a strong believer that nature tended to nurture those who embrace it. Nature sure did heal me that particular day. The redwoods were several years old. Visiting these trees almost felt like visiting my grandparents – those kind folks whom you often associated with for comfort. When things go wrong, they often come to your aid. That's precisely what the trees did. The gentle rustle of the leaves made me feel that they were offering kind words of comfort in their own tree language. It reminded me of the *Faraway Tree* series by Enid Blyton – a book that I often read as a little girl.

Later that evening, I was sitting inside my hotel room. Amit was watching television while Samara was playing with her dolls. I was browsing on my phone when I stumbled upon an update on the Ironman 70.3 Santa Rosa Facebook page. It said something about the probability of the swim section being cancelled due to fog. I read it three to four times to ensure that my eyes weren't playing tricks on me. I quickly alerted Amit who turned down the television volume.

"Look at this," I remarked.

Confused, he read the update.

I felt a swirl of emotions inside me. I got up and pranced around the room as my heart pounded loudly. Shaking my head, I wasn't sure whether to be elated or sad. The sudden rush of relief and happiness was interspersed with a feeling of guilt as I thought about the participants who had come for the race. Without the swim, the Ironman 70.3 wasn't really considered Ironman 70.3. No triathlon is complete without a swim. Supposing I was in a position where I could have done this, I would have been devastated of having the swim cancelled. I wouldn't have felt complete without the swim. The ghost of Ironman 70.3 would have continued to haunt me. It would have been a scenario of having done the race with an incomplete feeling.

Was this some sort of a message? A message that I was capable of doing the Ironman 70.3 race but maybe Santa Rosa wasn't meant for me. Probably I was meant to do some other Ironman 70.3 race. But which one? All of a sudden, the Ironman 70.3 Santa Cruz event instantly came to my mind. I had vaguely recollected the date to be sometime in September. At that time when I was signing up for Santa Rosa, I half wished that I could do Santa Cruz instead.

"Swe...," Amit began but I shushed him trying to gather my thoughts. It appeared as though Santa Cruz was in my destiny. I did my first Sprint distance triathlon there, my first Olympic distance in Capitola which was again a part of Santa county and now... maybe I might do my first Ironman 70.3 there. Suddenly it was all coming into place. When I came back from the bike ride at the camp dejected, Amit mentioned that we would be staying in the Bay area for some more time. Santa Cruz! Yes, that's it.

My heart did a leap and I did a jig around the room. Samara and Amit looked at me in surprise. I stopped and looked at both of them in delight. It felt as though a divine force injected some energy into my system. I felt like I had gulped down ten bottles of Gatorade. After walking around like a dead soul, I finally felt alive. That spark had returned and I was ready to take on any challenge. I quickly browsed through the Ironman website and clicked on Santa Cruz. The registration was still open.

"Swe what's going on?" Amit asked feeling perturbed.

"Don't you get it Amit? I was destined to do Santa Cruz."

He looked confused.

"Had I done the event tomorrow I wouldn't have had the satisfaction of doing Ironman 70.3?"

It suddenly dawned on Amit as I narrated my thoughts.

"Yes, I might be considered crazy. But I just have a strong feeling about this. Maybe this vacation was a break that was pushed upon us. For us to relax and unwind. To get back my energy and recover from the stress that we have been through past few months."

I pumped my fist in the air and announced, "I am signing up for Santa Cruz."

"Are you sure Swe?"

"Yes! I have never been so sure. Santa Cruz gave birth to a triathlete in me and this time it will give birth to an Ironman."

Amit saw the fire in my eyes – a spark that had almost diminished. He knew that look. It was a look that I possessed during my first half marathon back in 2012 and during my first Olympic distance last year with a bruised arm and knee.

"Okay... go ahead if you are sure."

Quickly I signed up for the event which was scheduled for September 9th, 2018. I then began to check for swim clinics at Cowell Beach. There was one next weekend for the Tri Santa Cruz event conducted by Penni. Déjà vu moment. It was exactly a year since I attended her clinic when I did my first Sprint distance triathlon. I quickly mailed Penni asking if she remembered me from last year and if there was room for one more participant. She replied warmly stating that she did remember me and I was welcome to attend the clinic.

I immediately dialled Viv's number and told him what had happened at Santa Rosa and how I signed up for Santa Cruz.

He was surprised but happy, "Alright I'll send you a plan. You have about six weeks."

I hung up feeling happier. I had something to look forward to.

Amit was still recovering from the sudden turn of events while Samara went back to playing with her dolls.

As I leaned back against my pillow, I couldn't help thinking about the contrast between my previous visit to Santa Rosa earlier this month and the current one. The earlier visit involved a vigorous training camp which I had taken part in with a fatigue-induced body. I had come back with a low self-confidence and bouts of low. While this current visit managed to induce that spark in me – enough to sign up for another Ironman 70.3 race.

A part of me felt guilty about feeling thrilled about the swim being cancelled. That disappeared over time as I began to read about the course at Santa Cruz. The swim was around the wharf, the bike was on Highway 1 and the run was the same as the Santa Cruz half marathon course. I had run the Santa Cruz Half Marathon in March and was familiar with the course. I remembered Emily telling me that the bike course wasn't hilly. My only worry was the ocean swim. Cowell Beach could get cold.

The television was blaring but I was in my own triathlon world. I went to the website of PacWest Endurance and signed up for the Ironman 70.3 Santa Cruz camp. This time I was determined to make my dream come true.

Chapter 14

A Blind Date with A Triathlon

*"If you set a goal for yourself and are able
to achieve it, you have won your race. Your goal
can be to come in first, to improve your performance,
or just finish the race it's up to you."*

— *Dave Scott*

I had never gone on a blind date. Signing up for the Olympic distance at the Oakland Triathlon felt like going on one. I was experiencing all the symptoms that one would on a blind date from what I have read. Nervous knots formed in my stomach and my throat felt dry. My heart felt as though there was a rock concert playing inside my system.

With my other triathlon events, I had always attended the one day swim clinics which enabled me to preview the swim and bike course. It gave me a psychological edge on race day. However, I couldn't attend the Oakland swim clinic due to unforeseen reasons.

After I had signed up for the Ironman 70.3 Santa Cruz, I was supposed to do another Olympic distance triathlon scheduled on August 12th. It was the Tri Santa Cruz event and was part of my training. Since the swim clinic at Oakland was on August 11th, I couldn't make it. Unfortunately, on the morning of August 12th, I had a vomiting bout – a result of a late night on Friday and not eating for long hours. I had to skip the Tri Santa Cruz race much to my dismay.

Fortunately, there was another Olympic distance triathlon the next Sunday, August 19th which was scheduled at Oakland. It was organized by USA Productions and just like their other events, they had no cut-off times. I instantly signed up for it and ensured that I rested and recovered the entire week. After all I had to swim 0.95 miles, bike 25 miles and run 6.2 miles again. If all goes well, this would be my fourth Olympic distance triathlon.

Oakland was situated on the east side of San Francisco Bay. The transition was on Webster Street. It was dark as I wheeled my bike into transition. Several athletes had already secured their spots. They were setting up their things and engaging in a lively chatter. I found a spot to rack my bike and began to set up my things. When I did, I ensured that I hadn't missed anything out. I looked around to see if I could spot a volunteer to get my body marked. That's when I saw Trish from PacWest. Greeting her with a hug, she began to write my age and bib number.

"So, you are doing the Olympic, right?" she asked.

I nodded.

"Well, good luck," she smiled.

I then spotted Coach Jay who was doing the announcements. I hugged him as well and he wished me good luck.

The darkness began to fade away giving room for daylight to seep in. I looked at the sky and mixed feelings began to coil in my heart. I had no idea about the course or how the event would go. Besides I was wearing my new tri-suit that read Ironman. The swim was in the Oakland estuary starting at the Jack London Aquatic Centre. I was told that the swim was along the current and one of the fastest swims. I walked barefoot to the swim start with a few other participants. I noticed a few of them place their shoes near the swim exit as it was supposedly a long transition from the swim exit to transition. I would have brought a pair too had I attended the swim clinic and understood the logistics.

Swim along the estuary – The walk to the swim start took forever. By the time I reached the start, I was warmed up. There was a huge board and athletes had to get into the water by jumping off the board. I jumped into the water. It was warm. I began swimming a few strokes to warm up before the race began. Other participants were warming up as well. Soon we were all huddling up together in the water as the race was about to begin. I took a deep breath and began to swim the strokes. The other participants raced ahead of me. I felt a sudden surge of panic seeing them go ahead. A fear that kept coming back to me time and again. It felt as though I'd be left alone to fend for myself in open waters. I knew it was a ridiculous thought as there were volunteers on kayaks stationed at regular intervals to ensure that I do not get left behind. I froze, gasped and spluttered. I tried to put my head down and swim but I began to pant heavily and lose breath. Why wasn't my swim showing any signs of improvement? I thought in despair. Do I need personalized coaching in swimming? Would I ever learn to put my head down and swim like other normal athletes? With such thoughts plunging my turbulent mind, I waded through the calm waters of the estuary. It seemed to go on forever. I swam with my head up. One of the volunteers suggested I put my head down in order to go faster. However, I had lost my rhythm by then. I struggled with my strokes and had half a mind to give up. The kind volunteer egged me on with encouraging words. I then saw that there were two other swimmers in the water. A sense of relief washed over me as I realized I wasn't the last one. Desperate to get out of the water, I swam as though I was trying to save my life. It was the longest swim and it seemed to take forever to get to the exit.

I passed a few boats and finally spotted the buoy from where we had to take a right turn to the swim exit. It was one of the most awkward exits where I had to be hauled up by a group of volunteers. It almost felt like being rescued from a storm. I struggled to climb up the boat as I was exhausted from the swim. When I finally got to my feet, I climbed up the ramp and took a right turn. I unzipped my wetsuit till waist down and continued running. My lungs and breath felt heavy as I edged forward. My legs felt wobbly and I tried to steady myself. I ran straight and took another left turn as guided by the volunteers. I had to cross the road, climb up four floors, cross the railway tracks, climb down the stairs and run to transition. By then I felt depleted of all my energy reserves.

I sure wasn't prepared for this transition which seemed to take forever. This entire stretch was counted as swim time. I had taken 70 minutes.

Transition 1: The toughest part of transition is getting out of your wetsuit. I struggled and pulled it out. I then slipped on my helmet, gloves and shoes. I was probably amongst the last. Trish cheered me on. I darted a grateful look at her. It helped that someone made you feel like a champion when you were feeling like a loser. I popped a Gu gel and wheeled my bike to the area which said mount bike. I had taken 7 minutes inside transition.

Bike ride on East Bay – While I was slow on the swim, I seemed to fly on my bike. It was slated as a fast and flat course on the website. It was a two-loop course and I was enjoying exploring the urban charm of Oakland on my bike. I passed cafés, walls with squiggles and managed to get a glimpse of the Bay Bridge at one point. I spotted a few other bikers and was glad to have some company. On my second loop, I had the race officials pull up next to me on their bike.

"Mam did you start late?"

I looked at them in confusion.

"Umm no," I replied wondering where this was heading. My chest began to tighten, thinking that they were going to disqualify me from the race.

"We will be closing the bike course shortly so bike as fast as you can."

Relief washed over me and I took a deep breath. "Got it," I said. I was confused wondering what was happening. I had read on the website which said that there were no cut-off times for any of the disciplines. Nevertheless, I continued biking.

My legs felt as though they had grown wings as I pedalled hard. The race officials were trailing me on their bike and it almost made me feel like royalty being escorted by security guards.

I noticed a few other bikers on the course. The competitive edge took over me as I pedalled past them, shouting "On your left." This was said to alert the biker in front of you in order to avoid a crash or an accident. Glad that I wasn't the last one, I breezed on the course until I reached transition. I dismounted from my bike and wheeled my bike to the spot. I glanced at my Garmin and saw that it was my fastest bike time in a triathlon. I was thrilled as I had completed my bike in 100 minutes.

Transition 2: I racked my bike, removed my helmet and gloves. I popped another Gu gel and picked up a bottle of Gatorade. Panting, I walked out of transition and was cheered by the volunteers. I took not more than a couple of minutes.

Run along Lake Merritt – My legs felt like bricks. It always did after the bike portion of the triathlon. It took me about 2 miles to get into rhythm. As I exited out of transition, I took a left, a right and entered the pathway that led to Lake Merrit. It was a beautiful place with tall, grey buildings overlooking the lake. There were several walkers and joggers on the pavement. It was noon and I was beginning to feel tired with the sun beating down hard. I kept taking walk breaks during my run. Since all my focus was on the swim and bike, I had lost my rhythm for the runs.

I spotted ducks floating peacefully on the lake. As I circled around the lake, I spotted a couple of homeless people. Feeling sorry for them, I kept moving on taking sips of Gatorade.

I popped another Gu gel at the 3 mile mark. I paused to take a breather and looked around. There were a few more runners on the course. I was once again glad not to be the last one. I continued running and soon reached the road near transition. Just as I thought I had reached the finish line, I was in for a rude shock. A kind faced volunteer said that I had to climb up those stairs, cross the railway tracks and then climb down again to run to the finish line.

I looked at him in disbelief and horror. "You are kidding," I muttered hoping that this was just a joke.

He shook his head and darted an empathetic look, "I know! It's hard, right?"

I nodded and went on to climb those four floors for the second time that day. Huffing and puffing, I hobbled across the tracks and climbed the stairs down.

"How far is the finish line?" I asked the volunteers stationed there breathlessly.

My legs felt wobbly, my breathing felt heavy and all I wanted was to just go back home.

"That way," she said pointing to the pathway.

I could hear the emcee's voice from a distance. Gathering all my reserves, I ran and ran till I reached the finish line. I had completed my fourth Olympic distance triathlon in 4:11:52.

I plonked on the ground and sat there for some time. I was happy to finish my fourth Olympic distance triathlon. It wasn't a great time but I felt stronger. I noticed someone smiling and coming towards me. It was Coach Char who came up to me and congratulated me. I mumbled thanks and expressed my concern about the swim and my inability to put my head in water.

"Don't worry. Just keep practicing," he assured me.

I then asked him about joining the triathlon programme with Team Asha and we exchanged email ids. I collected my finisher's medal and limped to transition to collect my bike and belongings. Amit and Samara couldn't accompany me this time. I had hired a vehicle so I called the driver. He was kind enough to help me with the bike and I sat on the back seat and drifted off to sleep.

I was exhausted but felt stronger than I had in days. The adrenalin rush of completing another triathlon began to seep into my veins. Oakland Triathlon was an urban triathlon in every way. Its rustic charm and the long transitions helped me build a solid foundation. Enough to give me confidence about my Ironman 70.3 race which was three weeks later. However, the following week, I had to survive the Ironman 70.3 Santa Cruz camp conducted by Coach Jay and PacWest team. I almost didn't.

Chapter 15

Swim with PacWest and Team Asha

"Each time we face our fear, we gain strength,
courage, and confidence in the doing."

— *Theodore Roosevelt*

There were just two weeks left for the Ironman 70.3 Santa Cruz race. It was the end of August and here I was at Depot Park along with the PacWest team. This time I was a lot more eager, energetic and upbeat. The weather, typical of Santa Cruz, was foggy and cold. Yet that failed to deter my spirits.

Coach Jay addressed all of us as we stood in a circle.

"Congratulations on your fourth Olympic," he smiled at me. I nodded and smiled back.

Then he went on to address the group. There were mostly people from the Santa Rosa camp along with a few additions.

He went on to explain about the activities lined up for

the day. "So, we would be swimming around the wharf, biking on Highway 1 and running along West Cliff Drive. I will be on the kayak."

It was later that day I'd realize the importance of swimming around the wharf.

Coach Jay remarked what a beautiful day it was to swim.

"Really?" I remarked as I was still not used to swimming in cold weather.

"It's a beautiful day. You are going to be fine."

We all headed towards the beach and warmed up for 10 minutes. Coach Jay got on his kayak. As we entered the waters, I noticed that the others were swimming fast and deftly, just like the triathletes that I had seen in the videos. As usual I was lagging behind at a snail's pace. Coach Jay was extremely patient with me throughout.

The cold water made me gasp and splutter every time I'd try and put my face into the water. It had been a year since I was swimming in open water. Yet I hadn't made any progress. What was wrong?

"Swetha, you are doing great," Coach Jay encouraged me.

I stopped to catch my breath. I held on to his kayak.

"Keep going. Don't stop."

"Coach. In the pool, I am fine. So why is it I struggle here?"

"Okay! Now just imagine that this is your pool. See

how calm the ocean is. That's right. This is your pool and you will swim all the way around the wharf."

I nodded, determined to make it.

I began to make an effort to put my head down and swim. This is my pool, I told myself repeatedly. I kept looking up to see if I had reached the end of the wharf. I heard sea lions barking. I froze and looked at Coach Jay in terror.

"I can't go any further," I panted.

"They won't harm you. Just keep going. You are swimming faster when you put your head down."

Once again, I began swimming my strokes. I had almost reached the end of the wharf. Just as I was about to give a pat on my back, I saw to my horror that the end of the wharf was deceptive. It was shaped like a hockey stick and seemed to keep going on forever. No wonder it was considered as an achievement to swim around the wharf. I paused and looked at Coach Jay in despair.

"You are doing great. In fact, I have to catch up with you."

I looked around at the shades of grey around me. The grey sky and the ocean. Everything was eerily quiet. It seemed as though the entire universe was watching me go through this survival test. Were they mocking me or looking at me with pity? One couldn't comprehend nature's capricious stance. I was panting and looked longingly at Coach Jay's kayak hoping to get a ride back.

"Keep going Swetha," Coach Jay encouraged me. "Keep sighting every three strokes."

Encouraged by his kind words, I finally made it to the other end.

Coach Jay called out, "You are almost there. Sight that white hotel in front and keep swimming towards it."

I nodded and paused to catch my breath before I dived into the waters again.

This was far better than the swim at Oakland. I guess that's what the presence of a coach like Jay does to you. You develop a little more confidence and a sense of determination.

I kept swimming with those occasional pauses and goaded by Coach Jay, I reached the shore in one piece.

"Way to go. You made it around the wharf."

I glanced at my watch which read 51 minutes for a mile. To my surprise it was faster than my pool time. There was a sudden spring in my step when I joined Trish and others. It gave me hope that I'd manage to make the swim cut-off.

I expressed this in glee to which Coach Jay said, "Of course, you'll make the swim cut-off. Why do you doubt that?"

I smiled as we all headed towards Depot Park to collect our bikes. Coach Jay explained the route and assigned pairs. I was once again paired with Tuan.

We set off along West Cliff Drive and took the

road that led to Highway 1. As I took a left turn, I pedalled hard with Tuan trailing behind me. I tried to keep up with the pack this time but they were quite fast.

It was a beautiful course. Highway 1 had spectacular views of the ocean and there were crosswinds. The course was hilly but they were more rolling hills. I shifted gears and all that biking at Santa Rosa had made me stronger.

"Just keep changing your gears," Tuan instructed.

It was probably the new surge in confidence after the Oakland triathlon. I was breezing on my bike this time. My bike Rocky was standing by me like a rock. I kept pushing even up the hills. I tried to avenge the ghosts of Santa Rosa by pedalling fiercely. I wasn't going to let the hills deter my dream, I thought.

I reached Davenport where Coach Jay greeted me, "You are doing great. In due time, you must switch to cleats," he said.

I nodded.

After waiting for Tuan, we again set off. It was more or less downhill and I soon found myself at Depot Park. It was a strong ride and I felt great. After a 3 mile run on West Cliff Drive, we wrapped up the camp and headed out to Ideal Bar & Grill for lunch.

Coach Jay addressed all our queries and wished us luck.

I went back home happier, but that little niggle of doubt wouldn't go away. I still felt wary of the ocean and the wharf swim. I felt I needed one more swim to elevate my confidence levels of making the swim cut-off.

When I went home that afternoon, I was greeted by Amit and Samara. We had shifted out of the Stanford Campus by then and moved into an apartment in Santa Clara. It was about 20 minutes away from Stanford.

"So how did it go," Amit asked.

I plonked myself on the sofa exhausted.

"Went well…," my voice trailed.

"I can see that you are a lot more confident."

Samara was drawing on a blank piece of paper. She was immersed in her little world of art and I watched her for a little while.

"Hmm I hope so. Well I guess I just need one more swim around the wharf."

Amit looked at me in surprise.

"Why what happened?"

"It is tricky around the wharf. Just one more swim, and I'll be fine."

We pondered over it for some time. The next weekend was Labour Day weekend and most people would be out. I was wondering if I could reach out to someone when I suddenly recollected my conversation with Coach Rajeev Char of Team Asha, post the Oakland triathlon event.

I had exchanged emails with him and I decided to reach out.

I received a positive reply saying that he would keep

me in the loop if he knew anyone who was going.

The following week, I received another mail from him where he had looped me with two other people – Kiran and Suryakant. We were to be joined by Deepa. After a few exchanges, we decided to meet at a local Starbucks joint and carpool from there.

On Labour Day weekend, I met Deepa, Kiran and Suryakant for the first time. They were warm and friendly and I instantly felt comfortable with them. We drove down to Santa Cruz in Kiran's car.

I expressed my fears and inhibitions to them. They assured me that I'll be fine. We slipped on our wetsuits at Depot Park. Grey seemed to be Santa Cruz's favourite colour. As usual it was cold and foggy. I dreaded having to enter the waters. With every step towards the water, I felt my stomach coiling into knots. I took a deep breath as terror washed over my eyes. The ocean was dangerously calm. We warmed up for 10-15 minutes. I still didn't feel ready for a long swim. Deepa noticed my fear and said that it'll be okay. We both discovered that we swam at a similar pace. Besides we would all watch out for one another. Keeping small goals, we decided to swim up to a certain point to ensure we were all fine before moving ahead.

I trailed behind Deepa. Coach Jay's words kept echoing in my mind, "This is your pool. Remember that." We reached the white buoy and paused.

"All good?" Deepa asked.

I nodded. We kept going. I was gasping and panting but ensured not to lose track of Deepa. I can do this, I told myself. We soon reached the wharf and this particular stretch felt long just as it had the previous week. It almost felt like I wasn't moving and just fighting the water. The sea lions were calm for a change, probably empathizing with me silently. I chanted my mantra again, pleading to God to help me get through the swim. Everything looked cold and grey around me. It appeared like a black and white sketch of an artist.

When I reached the end, I spotted the big white hotel on the shore. Once again, remembering Coach Jay's words about sighting the hotel, I began swimming my strokes. After a few struggles, I finally reached the shore along with Deepa. Suryakant and Kiran were already there and applauded us.

"Good going," they said.

I glanced at my watch which displayed a similar time as the previous week. I quickly estimated that I'd finish my swim in an hour at the event and felt relieved.

After enjoying a coffee break, we headed back home as a happier lot. There were a lot of jokes and laughter. I thanked each one of them profusely for the swim and mailed Coach Char as well stating the same.

It appeared as though I was all set. Amit had booked a room at the Ocean Pacific Lodge which was right opposite to Depot Park. We were to drive on Friday morning and come back on Sunday evening. Everything seemed to be going well so far. Yet I'd know the outcome only on Sunday which was just a few days away. For the rest of the nights, one question haunted me constantly – would I make the cut-offs and cross the finish line of Ironman 70.3?

Chapter 16

The Ultimate Final Test

*"Life is a race, and what matters most isn't when
a person crosses the finish line, but how strong
they've grown along the way."*

— *Jen Stephens*

When I got out of the water, I was just exhausted from reminiscing my last one year's journey. I was finally at the start line of the Ironman 70.3 race. The feeling was similar to the one that I had experienced when I stood at the full marathon start point at the Mumbai Marathon in January 2013. Someone had told me that it required immense courage to even get to this point. Those words came back to me when I headed towards the swim start today.

I smiled at other fellow participants and walked towards the swim start. There were volunteers holding placards with swim timings. I went and stood next to the one that read 50-60 minutes. On the way, I spotted Suryakant and Kiran and wished them luck. I couldn't spot Deepa anywhere. I was waiting for the race to begin in another ten minutes. The sun was already up at 6:50 am. What a pleasant change. All this while I had only been privy to the shades of grey. It was nice to see the contours of blue for once.

I was amidst all these athletes who looked like professionals in their wetsuits and swim caps. While they engaged in a friendly banter, I could detect a serious undertone.

"You know they pull you out of the water if you fail to make the cut-off within 70 minutes," said one man.

"Oh, that's pretty brutal," remarked another. "My friend failed to make the cut-off at Hawaii. The waves were rough apparently and she is a pretty good swimmer."

My self-confidence hit rock bottom. I wondered what would happen if I didn't make the cut-off. Alright! At least I had the guts to attempt something as daunting as this race, I comforted myself. The horn blew and it was time. Here goes, I thought closing my eyes and appealing to the forces of nature to help me get through this one. I began to chant my mantra.

Swim around sea lions – The start was initially crowded with the flurry of swimmers who entered around the same time. I tried dodging them half afraid that their legs may knock my goggles off, recollecting a horror story narrated by a triathlete at one of the training camps that I had attended. I shuddered at the thought of swimming without goggles in the ocean. The salt water could sting your eyes and make them feel as though they were on fire. I moved to the left hoping that the swimmers would go ahead. I kept my eyes occasionally on the orange buoys that were placed as markers around the entire course which was 1.2 miles.

"Remember when you put your head down, you will glide faster. And this is your swimming pool." Coach Jay's voice echoed in my ears. For the first time since I began my triathlon journey in 2017, I put my head inside the water. I had finally mustered enough courage to accept that I couldn't see anything below unlike in a swimming pool. To overcome this fear, I had devised a strategy.

Just a couple of days ago, I had watched *The Little Mermaid* animation with Samara. I recollected the ease with which Ariel – the mermaid glided amidst the waves. Of course, she had fins while I had to be content with just a pair legs. I decided to visualize the entire animation while putting my head down. To overcome the terror of being unable to see anything, my rapid imagination took over. I began to see Flounder, Ariel and her sisters and even Ursula – the sea witch. I imagined them waving at me and cheering me on. It helped me to continue swimming with my head down and not get psyched by the inability to see anything. The water was warmer and it helped me continue my swim in a rhythmic manner. Suddenly it sunk that I was at the Ironman swim. I was finally at the Ironman event. A shiver ran down my spine just thinking about the enormity of the brand. Ironman! Wow. On the other hand, this was Santa Cruz and in the past two weeks, it had almost become home for me.

I had reached the turning point of the wharf where I heard the sea lions bark loudly. They looked pretty well fed today, I thought glancing at them as I put up my head to breathe. For some reason, this part of the ocean was stinking this morning. The bad odour made me feel nauseous so I quickly swam to get to the turnaround point of the wharf. This portion was what I dreaded the most and the waves were quite choppy today. Such was the precarious nature of the ocean. Volunteers were hovering about on their kayaks.

I put up my head and asked, "Which way?" for a minute, I was confused and worried that I had steered off course.

"Just follow the swimmers," one of them replied gesturing towards some.

Following them, I finally made the turn around and could spot the white hotel at a distance. I used that as my sighting point and began to swim towards it.

A sudden wave of fatigue hit me and I began to feel out of breath. I lifted my head up to inhale some fresh air.

"Are you alright?" a volunteer on the kayak asked. I

nodded and glanced at my Garmin watch. I just had 0.25 miles to go. Swimming towards the shore was relatively easy as the waves sort of aided you, eager to get you out of their abode. "Come, move out," they seemed to say gently. The shore was drawing closer and before I realized, I was home. I crossed the timing mat in 00:59:50. Way ahead of the cut-off time which was 70 minutes. I felt a wave of relief wash over me. I did it! A huge weight had been lifted off my shoulders when I crossed the first hurdle.

I unzipped my wetsuit from behind, pulled the sleeves off my arms and let it hang waist down while I ran towards Depot Park to get my bike.

"Well done Swe," Amit remarked from the stands while Samara chirped saying, "Mama you are a champion."

"Swetha, you were amazing." I looked up to see Penni smiling at me. I paused and hugged her with gratitude recollecting my very first open water swim with her on this same beach a year ago. "Now go kill it on the bike," she patted me.

I nodded and ran into the transition.

Transition 1: The hardest part of a triathlon was getting out of the wetsuit. So, I let the volunteers help me take it off. I stood there dripping wet in my tri-suit which I had worn beneath my wetsuit. The bike stands were relatively empty, as the faster swimmers were already on the bike course. I could easily spot my Rocky – my bike. I rushed towards it, throwing my cap, goggles and wetsuit into the spare plastic bag.

Slipping on my helmet, biking glasses and shoes, I tied my race bib belt around my waist. Panting slightly, I stuffed few packets of Gu gels into my pockets behind the tri-suit. Each energy gel packet contained 100 calories and would help me sustain myself on that bike for 56 miles. I wheeled my bike that had two bottles of Gatorade – a sports drink, attached to the holder below my seat. I reached the point that said, 'Mount Bike Here'. I was shaking with nervousness as I glanced at my watch. I had taken 11 minutes and now had just 4 hours and 20 minutes to finish my bike course. Muttering a silent prayer, I mounted on my bike and set off.

Riding the wheels on Highway 1 – My legs were initially wobbly due to my heart rate which had suddenly shot up. I had to initially climb a slope which led to West Cliff Drive. I was panicking and breathing heavily as a hurricane of thoughts was slowly forming in my head. What if I get a flat tyre? I don't even know how to fix one. I remember learning it once but it was such a complicated procedure that trigonometry seemed like a baby in comparison.

The initial 6 miles till the Highway was a flat course. I soon reached the point where I had to take a left on Highway 1. It wasn't closed for traffic but being a Sunday there were lesser number of cars on the road. Of course, there were volunteers and aid stations at different points. The combination of headwinds and hills put a strain on my legs. While pedalling uphill, I was met with a lot of resistance. It appeared as though the winds were playing a sadistic game with me. "Get past us," they seemed to say and the rolling hills were getting bigger with every mile. By now, my lungs were deprived of oxygen and my quads were on fire. "Stop don't torture us," they seemed to say.

I reached Davenport which was at the 12th mile. I paused on the side of the road and took a few sips from my Gatorade bottle. I had seen a lot of bikers drink from their bottles while riding. I had tried doing that once only to have a bad fall. I didn't want to take that chance again. Not with those monstrous headwinds which were ready to throw me off my bike any moment. I glanced at my small computer device attached in between the handlebars on the bike. It was called the element bolt which displayed speed, time and distance and wattage. The speed displayed 12.7 mph. At this rate, I wouldn't make the bike cut-off I thought ruefully. Just like I comforted myself earlier, I told myself that it was better to have tried than not tried at all. I will keep going as far as I could until the race officials decide to pull me off the course.

I saw many bikers going past calling out, "On your left" indicating that they were going to overtake me. My spirits sank further. They were zooming on their bikes while in comparison I was crawling like a tortoise. I reached the first aid station at mile 15. The tables had a lavish spread of oranges, nuts, energy cliff bars, Gu gels, water and some Gatorade. Wow! It looked like a feast. I stocked myself with bananas and Gu gels.

"You got this one," the volunteer remarked. Gaining some energy with those refreshments, I continued pedalling hard.

The ocean views were breathtaking and I had a hard time taking my eyes off them. It had become quite hot by now. The pristine blue pacific glistened in the bright sunlight causing slight ripples as the waves crashed on the shores. I saw bikers coming on the other side and they were on their way to transition. Lucky them. I'd do anything to be in their shoes now, I thought. To my right, I spotted some fields. There was a board that read Pie Ranch and immediately my stomach growled just thinking of pies. It hit me that I hadn't had anything to eat besides Gatorade, water and energy gels. The rolling hills were never ending and I continued pushing hard. After a while, I spotted the Pigeon Point Lighthouse to my left. This was the turnaround point at the 28th mile. When I reached there, I spotted one of the race officials, noting something on a piece of paper. My heart stopped and I became stiff wondering if I was going to be pulled off course.

Instead he remarked saying, "You got to go faster than you got here. Catch the tail wind while going back."

I nodded, grateful for the advice. I turned my bike and pedalled hard. I saw the speed go up to 13.7 mph on the bolt. While the rays of the sun beat down hard, I managed to glimpse a ray of hope. Maybe I could just make it. I stopped at the aid station at mile 30.

"Hot day, isn't it?" I remarked to the volunteers.

They agreed.

"Thank you, guys. You are doing a wonderful job," I expressed my gratitude while refilling my bottle of Gatorade.

Without them, I'd have probably fainted on the Highway. Just then I spotted a few bikers on the other side. They were far behind me, slower than I was. I felt a sense of relief knowing that I wasn't the last one. Another 26 miles to go. This was just a mile more than the biking distance for the Olympic distance triathlon. I had done this distance four times in the past. Come on, I told myself.

As the man had rightly said, the tailwinds were giving me an easier time. They seemed to aid me just like the waves did while I was swimming back to the shore. Perhaps both these forces of nature have their own way of making it up to us for giving us a hard time initially.

Nothing had gone wrong so far. I glanced up at the sky and chanted my mantra repeatedly – *Om Gan Ganapatayeh Namaha*. It was a belief that if you prayed to him before doing anything, he would prevent any kind of obstacles that was likely to come between you and your goal. At this point, I sincerely prayed that no obstacle would come in my way and that I'd reach Depot Park in one piece.

At one point, I found myself alone on Highway 1. Triathlon was a lonely sport in that sense. While you have volunteers cheering for you, you had to survive the entire ordeal all alone. Such instances could probably drive you mad to an extent that you start talking to yourself. In my case I began conversing with my bike Rocky. Rocky had seen me through five triathlon events in the past. It had never let me down so far. "Good old Rocky," I patted the handlebars. True to its name, it had stood rock solid by me during tough times. Probably more than any friend in the past did.

"Come on Rocky. You are doing great. Let us finish this together, shall we? Please don't let me down this time. I have dreamt of attaining the identity of Ironman 70.3 title for months now. You remember how we both had a tough time at Santa Rosa couple of months ago?" I pleaded with my bike. Of course, it couldn't hear me but just the thought of pouring my heart out made me feel lighter. I soon reached the last aid station at mile 48.

"You are doing great," the volunteers remarked, "you are almost there. Just 8 to go."

Experiencing a sudden rush of energy with those energy gels, I zoomed for 2 miles before I took a right turn on to a road that would lead me to Depot Park. I could spot people already running. It gave me a sudden surge of panic. My heart started beating fast realizing I still had 13.1 miles to run. I had a lot of catching up to do. It was then that Coach Emily's words came back to me, "Remember it's your race. You don't look at what others are doing and let that bog you down." Taking a deep breath, I decided to finish my bike leg strong. While runners were running on one side, there were families walking lazily with their strollers. A couple of people stood right in the middle of the road chatting and I literally had to bellow my lungs out.

"Behind you. Look out."

They scurried away like frightened rabbits and made way. Meanwhile I pedalled like a possessed person until I reached Depot Park in 4:02:41. Yes, I had made the cut-offs again. My joy knew no bounds. Tears stung my eyes and my heart was beating rapidly as I realized that I was just 13.1 miles away from achieving my dream. I felt lighter when I realized that I had crossed another hurdle.

"Way to go Swe," Amit shouted and Samara waved.

Transition 2: "Good job!" a volunteer said and gestured me to get off my bike. I dismounted and wheeled it to my rack. I took off my helmet and gloves, drank some water and popped another Gu gel. My legs felt like a ton of bricks from all that pedalling. It was 12:20 noon and was scorching hot. It felt like being trapped inside a microwave oven. I slipped on my cap which read Ironman. It took me around 5-6 minutes before I could venture out on my run. So, I now had 3 hours and 10 minutes to finish 13.1 miles of running.

Run: The route was the same as the one in the Santa Cruz Half Marathon which I had run in March. Little did I realize that running that event would come in handy. Initially I was supposed to do the Napa Valley Marathon on the same day in March. Unfortunately, due to that ankle injury, I shelved plans and ran the Santa Cruz Half Marathon instead. It seemed that I was preordained to do the Ironman 70.3 Santa Cruz race.

Three fourth of the course was on a trail with a good number of inclines. It was hard to run after spending four hours on the bike. My legs felt like jelly and for the initial mile, I walked more than I ran, trying to normalize my heart rate and catch my breath.

The run was along West Cliff Drive with scintillating views of the ocean and sand. The sheet of blue stretched along the sands with the white sails bouncing off the waves occasionally. I noticed a lot of runners returning from the run and heading towards the finish line. I felt another surge of panic. I began to focus on finding my rhythm. The first 3-4 miles were on a gradual incline before it ventured into Wilder Ranch State Park. I stopped at every aid station every 2 miles and poured water on my head. I was tired, hot and hungry. Being a runner for the last six years, my past experiences came in handy, making me touch mile 6 soon. I was relieved to have reached almost half point.

The dirt roads on the trail had a lot of stones. I had to tread cautiously on these so that I did not trip and fall. On my right, the ocean views were mesmerizing and the waters twinkled in the sunlight. I watched some surfers and families with dogs playing on the beach. I felt a twang of envy wishing I was out there lazing around instead of putting myself through this gruelling task. Just then I noticed a bare-chested runner behind me.

"Hey, are we on the right track?" he asked.

For a moment, my heart skipped a beat. Oh no! What if I had taken the wrong turn? Then I realized that I had been following the arrows marked on the course, diligently.

"Yes of course," I replied confidently.

"Glad to hear. I wouldn't want to get lost here," he grinned.

I smiled and went ahead.

I soon reached the 10th mile mark and by now I was ready to give up. Just then a volunteer waved her hands from a distance and gestured frantically. As I went closer, I realized she was trying to tell me that I just had 3 miles to the finish line. Fortunately, it was downhill so I tried to run with whatever energy I had left. I felt good overtaking few runners and could soon spot the beach. At mile 12, I could vaguely hear the emcee's voice. With every stride, my heart pounded. Just a few yards from the finish line, I spotted Amit who handed over me our country's flag. "You are there Swe," he exclaimed excitedly.

Holding the tri-coloured flag high, I crossed the finish line and was met with cheers and hoots from onlookers. I had made it! I had done it! With tears rolling down my cheeks, I plonked on the sand. A kind volunteer garlanded the Ironman 70.3 medal around my neck. I just crossed the finish line of IRONMAN 70.3 in 8 hours and 5 minutes!

At the finish – "Mama, you are a champion," Samara flung her tiny arms around me. Amit engulfed me into a big hug!

"Congrats Swe! You did it! I knew you would." His face portrayed a picture of happiness and pride. "This really calls for a celebration."

For a long time, I sat near the volunteer's station. I pinched myself several times to ensure it wasn't a dream.

"Did I really finish the Ironman 70.3 race?" I found myself asking a volunteer.

"You sure did and with a lot of time to spare before the cut-off," she smiled.

I glanced at my Ironman medal. It had a surf board engraved on it that read Ironman 70.3 Santa Cruz. It said 1.2 miles swim, 56 miles biking and 13.1 miles running. I clutched my medal, looked at the sky and offered a prayer of gratitude. After a while, I got up and hobbled to a place where I could click a picture of myself with the medal.

"You are limping," Amit remarked. His voice was drowned by the emcee's booming voice, constantly announcing the finishers' names. Despite the fact that I was limping, I held my head high flaunting my medal. When strangers began to congratulate me, my heart did a little jig. I felt like a champion. The feelings were similar to what I had experienced during my first Olympic distance triathlon which was incidentally a beach finish as well. My dream began to sink in slowly. Relief and elation washed over me as tears began to sting my eyes. It wasn't because of the pain even though my body ached.

I trotted to Depot Park to collect my bike and belongings. The staff at the Ocean Pacific Lodge had been kind enough to allow a late check out. I sat on the bed for a moment to gather my breath and thoughts. I hungrily munched on a burrito that Amit had bought for me while Samara repeatedly kept calling me 'Champion' in her endearing manner.

After a quick shower, I packed my belongings and loaded them into the car. When I went over to the reception to hand over the keys, the receptionist smiled at me.

"Congratulations! You did it," she exclaimed excitedly.

"Thanks," I smiled back.

"So, you will be coming back next year?"

I paused and reflected back to my thoughts when I had finished my race. I thought to myself that I would never ever do another 70.3 race again. I wasn't going to put myself through that gruelling torture or training regime. It was brutal. However, when I met the receptionist's eye, I surprised myself with an unexpected response.

"Yes!" I said with a lot more confidence than I had when I checked in couple of days ago. "I will be coming back for the race next year." I barely recognized my own voice. Was this what finishing one Ironman 70.3 race did to you? Made you believe in your capabilities a lot more? Maybe it did.

"Well. Good for you. See you next year," she said smiling.

"See you!"

For the first time since I landed in California, I felt a sense of accomplishment. I had managed to carve a new identity for myself – that of an Ironman or rather Ironwoman! I wasn't just a partner at the B School Community anymore. I had left my life at Stanford behind and was ready to start a new one. I had finally conquered my fear of open water swim and laid the inner demons to rest. I finally considered myself worthy of something. My shoulders no longer slouched and my gait was steady when I walked towards the car.

On the ride back home, I watched the sun sink slowly behind the clouds. The sky had a radiant glow. I realized that what I had achieved was just the beginning of a milestone. I definitely had miles to go before I sleep....

Acknowledgement

This book would not have been possible without the help of some good Samaritans, my publishers – Anup, Rinky, Manish, editor Vandana, entire Crossword and TheWritePlace team.

First, I thank God, my parents, my husband Amit and daughter Samara for really being supportive of my dreams. Coach Viv for always being just a phone call away and for making me believe in myself. I heartily thank one of my mentors Ashok Someshwar from Mumbai Road Runners for again being just a phone call away and encouraging me always.

Coach Penni for being patient with me during my first open water swim clinic at Cowell Beach. Coach Char for encouraging me during my first swim and putting me in touch with folks for that last swim before my Ironman 70.3 event.

I warmly thank the race director of Tri Santa Cruz event for allowing me to continue the event despite having lost my timing chip. Mermaid Series for putting up a great show and encouraging all newcomers like me to realize their dream of being a triathlete. My sincere gratitude to Coach Jay and Emily Ridgeway for those kind words of encouragement, especially Coach Jay who was patient with me during my first swim around the wharf. Thanks to the entire PacWest team who are a group of amazing people. USA Productions for having a great support system and enabling new triathletes to pursue their goals. Team Asha for accompanying me on the Labour Day weekend swim. A big thanks to the Mumbai Road Runners' Community for being encouraging of my runs, triathlon events and write-ups.

I also thank my old Coach Rama who was there for me during my lowest phase in July 2018, all my trainers at Five Fitness who reiterated the importance of strength training. It is this strength that made me reach the finish line of a gruelling race. I heartily thank Bike Connections for a great job with their servicing and tune ups of my bike.

Most importantly, I want to express my sincere gratitude to all my professors at Stanford creative writing courses for encouraging me to write an honest memoir, and also to all my classmates for providing valuable feedback. Without you guys, writing this memoir wouldn't have been possible.

About the Author

A journalist by profession, Swetha Amit, with a double Master's Degree in Psychology, has pursued Creative Writing courses at Stanford University, California. An avid reader, with a keen eye for specializing in books and reviewing, she is credited with more than 100 interviews of several best-selling authors around the world across a varied genre and many senior business leaders.

Swetha started her fitness journey as a marathoner, participating in numerous running events both in India and United States, and now pursues the sport called Triathlon. She has completed two Ironman 70.3 races and several Olympic distance triathlons in the United States.

She has been an event ambassador for running events in India and for the Oakland Triathlon, one of the largest urban triathlons in the world, in 2019. She also enjoys penning down her experiences and musings on her blog. As a writer, she has written articles for *Tell Me Your Story*. She currently resides in California with her husband and daughter.

Elated after making it through my first open water swim in icy waters of Cowell Beach. A big step towards overcoming a major hurdle in my triathlon journey.

Waving to Amit after finishing my swim in my very first triathlon event and flaunting my new wetsuit. I was relieved and tired at the same time.

I was just a few yards away from the finish line of my first triathlon! There was a spring in my step along with a surge of adrenaline rush.

The first of anything is always special! My first triathlon medal and a beautiful one too! A visible proof that my first 'Tri' wasn't a dream.

Acquainting myself with the open waters again during the second open water swim clinic at Capitola Beach. I was feeling strong and confident. Strong enough to take a step further in my triathlon journey.

Crossing the finish line at the Mermaid Series on Capitola Beach. Doing an Olympic distance triathlon was big for me. This accomplishment made me pose with my country flag.

Feeling jubilant after finishing my first Olympic distance triathlon at the Mermaid Series. Despite the physical bruises on my knee and arm, I felt strong enough to lift my bike.

One of my favourite medals even today. A beautifully carved medal in the shape of a mermaid. I was officially a Mighty Mermaid and a triathlete!

Thrilled after finishing my Olympic distance duathlon at Morgan Hill post the winter season. Setting the tone for a good triathlon season ahead.

With the PacWest team after a swim around the Santa Cruz wharf and sea lions! All smiles after surviving the training swim two weeks before the Ironman 70.3 event.

Coming out of the swim at the Ironman 70.3 race in 59 minutes.
I had made the swim cut-off! First hurdle out of the way.

Yes! I had made the swim cut-off at the Ironman 70.3 race at Santa Cruz! I was greeted by Penni who helped me during my first open water swim at this same place. Life comes a full circle!

Biking down to Depot Park at the Ironman 70.3 race. Another hurdle crossed and cut-off met. Relief and elation as I was inching closer to my dream!

After crossing the finish line of the Ironman 70.3 race with the Indian flag.
Wow! I actually accomplished what I thought was impossible!
A moment of pride, jubilance and disbelief.

Posing with my family who had been pillar of support throughout the journey after the Ironman 70.3 race. Celebration time with Amit and Samara!

A prized possession of mine and remains close to my heart! A proof that I am Ironwoman and that my dream became a reality!

Printed in Great Britain
by Amazon